THEN AND THERE SERIES
GENERAL EDITOR
MARJORIE REEVES, M.A., PH.D.

# Pioneers in the American West 1780-1840

BARBARA CURRIE, B.A.

MUSCROFT COUNTY SECONDARY SCHOOL
MONKSCROFT WAY
PRINCESS ELIZABETH
CHELTENHAM
PITVILLE SCHOOL

LONGMAN

LONGMAN GROUP LIMITED
London

*Associated companies, branches and representatives throughout the world*

© *Longman Group Limited (formerly Longmans,*
*Green & Co. Ltd) 1969*

*First published* 1969
*Second impression* 1970

ISBN 0 582 20454 2

*Printed in Malta by St Paul's Press Ltd*

ACKNOWLEDGEMENTS

We are grateful to the following for permission to reproduce copyright material: Holt, Rinehart & Winston Inc. for their arrangement of 'Roulant ma Boule' from *Ecouter et Chanter* by Klinck and Klinck; and Hudson's Bay Record Society for extracts from the thirteenth and twenty-third volumes (Peter Skene Ogden's Snake Country Journals, 1824-6 and 1826-7).

We are grateful to the following for permission to reproduce photographs: Bradford Angier, page 31; *The Beaver* (Hudson's Bay Company magazine), pages 27, 28-29, 30 top, 46 and 83; the Bobbs-Merrill Company Inc, from *Jedediah Smith and the Opening of the West* © 1953 by Dale L. Morgan, page 51; British Museum, pages 17, 18 left and right, 19 left and right; Department of Indian Affairs and Northern Development, page 11; Geological Survey of Canada, page 9; John Patrick Gillese, page 10; Hudson's Bay Company, pages 30 bottom and 45; the Mansell Collection, pages 33 and 84 (courtesy of the New York Public Library, Astor Lenox and Tilden Foundations); National Film Board of Canada, page 12 bottom; National Museum of Canada, page 8; National Park Service, Yellowstone National Park, Wyoming, pages 3, 4 and 5; New York Historical Society, page 74; Northern Natural Gas Company Collection, Joslyn Art Museum, pages 69 and 73; Oregon Historical Society, pages 42, 47, 50, 79 and 80; Paul Popper Ltd, pages 6 and 12 top; Radio Times Hulton Picture Library, page 39; Library of the State Historical Society of Colorado, page 80; Walters Art Gallery, page 65.

We have been unable to trace the Fine Arts Press, formerly of Santa Ana, California for permission to reproduce the illustration on page 37 from M. Sullivan *Travels of Jedediah Smith*, and apologize for any infringement of copyright.

# Contents

# To the Reader

One of the first things that the French and British settlers in America learned from the Indians was to hunt and trap animals for their meat and skins. They did this first for their own use and then began to send the furs across the Atlantic to Europe. The Company of the Adventurers of England Trading into Hudson Bay had been given a royal *charter* in 1670 to trade in and govern all the lands whose rivers ran into Hudson Bay. British settlers along the eastern coast of North America traded furs from the Indians. Frenchmen from Canada on the St Lawrence river travelled on the Great Lakes to the plains beyond, as far as the foothills of the Canadian Rockies and the Black Hills of Dakota. From their other colony of New Orleans Frenchmen had gone up the Mississippi and the lower part of the Missouri and they had been joined in this by Spaniards from their colonies of Mexico and Florida. Fur had always been profitable because clothes lined or trimmed with fur were a sign of wealth and success, much as a mink coat is today. From the seventeenth century onwards, felt hats made from beaver fur were popular. That is why the traders thought beaver skins one of the most valuable to buy.

The whole history of this trade would take a far bigger book than this. North America covers many millions of square miles. You could put Britain three times over into Oregon in 1840 and still have some land left over round the edges. The fur trade lasted several hundred years, so this book tells only part of the story.

It covers the time from when the English won Canada (1763) and lost the American colonies (1783) until the 1840s when the trade began to be less profitable, and it covers the space from the Mississippi westwards. The traders, in searching for furs, were also explorers, sometimes by accident, sometimes from curiosity. Some of them, like David Thompson, drew maps and some passed on their information to the surveyors who later mapped western America. Much of the book is about their journeys and, to understand them properly, you need bigger maps of the areas shown in this book. If you can, look up the places mentioned in a big atlas.

Most of the information in this book comes from the journals (or diaries) and letters of the traders themselves. Hudson's Bay Company officers had to keep journals and write reports of their work and many American trappers kept diaries. As you will see, their spelling and punctuation was not always as good as it might be, but perhaps if you have trouble with this yourselves, you can sympathise. It has not been corrected, so you can read what they actually wrote. Many of the trappers left no record because they could not read or write. Jim Bridger could not, though he could draw accurate maps in the sand, and Kit Carson learned to write only in the last few years of his life. Many travellers who were not trappers went to the mountains; Englishmen like George Ruxton to hunt, naturalists to study plants and animals, missionaries to convert Indians and artists to draw them, and people with lung trouble to recover their health in the pure mountain air. They too wrote descriptions of what they saw. There was nothing wrong with their spelling but they were a good deal more long-winded than the trappers, as you will see.

Words printed in *italics* are explained in the Glossary (p. 90).

# 1 The Hunting Grounds

In 1783 when the Americans won their independence from Britain, the British still held the Hudson Bay lands, run by the fur company, and the Canadian colony on the St Lawrence which they had won from the French in 1763. By the peace treaty with Britain, the new United States held all the land up to the Mississippi and in 1804 Thomas Jefferson, the American President, added to this Louisiana, which he bought from the French Emperor, Napoleon. From the map you can see that this was a very large stretch of land, although nobody was sure how large because it had not then been mapped. It meant that the way lay open to the Americans who were eager to move west to trade, where they would meet the British and Canadians who were already there.

This did not mean that the way was easy. Beyond the settled frontier were thousands of miles of rough country where the fur-bearing animals were to be found. From Hudson Bay or the St Lawrence the trader would travel over a country of lakes, rivers, forests, rocks and swamps. Even today it takes a train thirty hours to go from Montreal to Winnipeg and, north of the Great Lakes, it still passes through this rocky, forested land where no crops grow. This country was hot in the short summer and swarmed with black fly and mosquitoes, which tormented the trappers so much that they looked forward to the winter, although there might then be fifty or sixty degrees of frost and the lakes and rivers would freeze in November and not thaw again until April.

Stretching from this area in Canada west and south into the lands of the United States were the prairies and plains, crossed by rivers running from west to east into the Mississippi. The

*Yellowstone Lake*

greatest of these rivers was the Missouri but the Platte, the Arkansas and Red Rivers and many others would make even the Thames look very small. The prairies in the lower Missouri and Platte valleys, rolling grassland dotted with clumps of trees and shrubs and crossed by creeks bordered with cottonwoods, were compared by one English traveller to the parks of a country house, the work of *Capability Brown*.

Further west on the great plains there were very few trees, only short grass and less water, and further south these plains between St Louis and Santa Fe became arid deserts. The next obstacle to the traveller was the barrier of the Rocky Mountains, stretching from the far north in Canada to Mexico and with only a few easy passes through them. The Continental Divide in the Rockies separated the rivers like the Saskatchewan and Missouri which flowed eastwards, from the rivers like the Fraser, the Columbia, and the Colorado, which flowed into the Pacific. The scenery and the climate of the Rockies varied 3

*A geyser in Yellowstone park; first described by a trapper.*

from place to place. In places there were pleasant sheltered valleys with good grass and plenty of trees and animals. South Park or the Bayou Salade in Colorado was a valley like this and the trappers' descriptions of it made it sound like Paradise. But there were also rocky barren precipices where only a few pine trees grew and the snow was eight feet deep in winter. In these mountains, trappers saw strange rock formations, *petrified* trees and hot springs. They were not always believed when they told people back east about them. One trapper described the boiling springs of the Yellowstone as a 'number of hot and boiling springs some of water and others of most beautiful fine clay and resembles that of a mush pot and throws its particles to the immense height of twenty to thirty feet'.

Many early travellers thought that once over the Rockies they would not be far from the Pacific, but in between were hot dry deserts in the south and wide dry plains covered with *wormwood* and *sage-brush* further north. Even when these had been crossed there were still more mountains, the Sierra

*The Snake river and the Tetons; a trappers' landmark.*

Nevada, before they reached California, or the Blue mountains before they reached Oregon. On the Pacific side the mountains came very close to the sea in some places while in others there were fertile valleys like the Sacramento and the Willamette. The climate was more *temperate* in northern California and Oregon but traders on the Columbia river often had to endure heavy and continuous rain. The Indians on that coast had thought out how to make a waterproof shirt of a sea-lion's intestines to keep off the rain.

Many of the early travellers in these lands described the trees, the plants and the swarms of animals and birds they saw there. On the Pacific slopes there were fir trees and redwoods bigger than they had ever seen before. They found amongst the tangled undergrowth of the valleys of streams, dense bushes of honeysuckle, wild roses and different kinds of berries. David Thompson listed fourteen different kinds, including currants, raspberries and blue berries, a welcome source of food for Indians and trappers but also for grizzly bears, so they had to take care

5

*Yosemite Valley.*

they were not sharing a patch with one of them. In summer in the prairies and mountain valleys there were hundreds of different kinds of wild flowers, some like the *camas* with roots that could be eaten. Peter Ogden, a Hudson's Bay Company trader, said one day that 'in this day's Journey a Botanist would have had full employment', and later many botanists did travel with the trappers to make collections and records of all these plants.

## 2 The Animals

In most parts of this country, where there was water, were the animals the trappers were looking for, either for their fur or their meat or both. Along the rivers and streams were the beaver, the otter and musk-rat which they valued most, especially the beaver. Some beaver lived in the banks of streams but most built 'lodges' or homes in the water. They often dammed streams first by cutting down trees with their sharp teeth to fall across the stream, though they were not as clever at getting these in exactly the right place as is sometimes thought. The streams they dammed often spread over the land to make swamps, the water would no longer be deep enough

*Drift wood snags in the Missouri river.*

for them and they would start all over again in a new stream. Trappers found these swamps very difficult to cross. The beaver made their lodges with sticks, poles and brush wood, plastered together with mud carried between their fore-paws while they walked on their webbed hind feet. Their wide flat tails helped them to balance. They fed on the bark of leaves of aspen, willow or cottonwood, so whenever a trapper saw a stream bordered with these he hoped to find beaver lodges.

His traps were made of steel or iron with a chain which was attached to a strong stick driven into the stream bed. The trap was below the water but a little way above it was a twig baited with castoreum. This was a substance taken from the beavers' glands and mixed with cloves and cinnamon or some other strong smelling spice. The beaver would reach up to get this, his hind feet would be caught in the trap and he would drown.

*Beaver.*

*A beaver dam.*

The position of the trap was marked by a floating stick. The trapper waded into the stream to set the trap and collect the animals, an unpleasant job in winter which was the best time to trap as the animal had a thick coat for the winter. Rheumatism was an *occupational disease* with trappers.

The beaver was skinned, its skin scraped, dried on a wooden frame and then folded up, fur side in. If cleaned very carefully, the furs were more valuable. Indian women were very good at this. Ogden said once that the 'ladyes of the Camp' were *'vieing with* each other who will produce . . . the cleanest and best dress'd beaver'. The Company would pay an extra shilling for carefully cleaned skins. The skins were made up into bundles, pressed together and tied with cords.

Skins of the deer were also valued to make leather. There were many animals of the deer family from the caribou and moose of the north to the mule deer, white tail elk and antelope further south. The *elusive* mountain goat was really an antelope. The big-horn sheep were hunted for their meat and skin but as

*Grizzly bear.*

they could climb fast and up the steepest precipices they were hard to catch.

Bears were killed for their skins, meat and fat which could be melted down and used as a substitute for butter. Black and brown bears were harmless enough unless wounded or very hungry but grizzly bears were often killed in self-defence. These were the largest and fiercest of the mountain bears. They might measure up to nine feet in length and weigh eight hundred pounds. Their fur was brownish and flecked with white hairs or grizzled, which was how they got their name. It was so dangerous to hunt them, especially with bow and arrow or spear, that if an Indian killed one he wore its teeth as a necklace to show his bravery.

The only other animal which would attack men, if it was hungry enough, without being attacked first was the cougar or mountain lion, but this was a wary animal rarely seen. A fully grown cougar would measure nine feet from head to tail and it could climb, so it was no good getting up a tree to escape it, as trappers did with grizzly bears. Wolves and coyotes were not dangerous but they were a nuisance as they carried off meat stored by the trappers and, if hungry in winter, would attack their horses or even drag away their saddles to chew the leather.

The smaller animals escaped the Indians and trappers unless they were hungry. There were many different kinds of rabbits, hares and squirrels. One of the squirrel family attracted the attention of all the travellers. This was the prairie dog, a ground squirrel which lived in 'towns', collections of burrows dug up into mounds two or three feet high. Sentinels stood at the doors of these houses to give warning of an enemy's approach with a volley of chattering which sounded enough like a bark to give them their name. Prairie owls and rattlesnakes also lived in these towns, but whether to prey on them or for company, nobody seemed very sure. Rattlesnake bites could be fatal but,

*Buffalo.*

*Prairie dogs.*

*Mountain goat.*

if alarmed, the snakes made a whirring noise with the rings of scales or rattles with which their bodies were covered and so a man could avoid them. All the other snakes found in the west were harmless.

The animal which was valued by Indians and whites alike for food was the buffalo or bison. Millions of these roamed the western plains and the valleys of the Rockies, often travelling in enormous herds. With its huge shaggy head and shoulders, short legs, small body and little tail, it was not beautiful but it was very useful. In fact the horse and the buffalo together were the whole livelihood of the Plains Indians.

## 3 The Indians

The Plains Indians were the first that the traders met beyond the Mississippi valley and the Red River of the North. Although they grew some crops, most of these were hunters living on meat. Their women gathered roots and berries. Each tribe had a stretch of territory which might be seven or eight hundred miles in extent. The tribes knew the boundaries and they kept within them unless they were fighting a war, stealing horses or trading with other tribes. Within their territory most of them followed the buffalo though some of them, like the Mandans and Arikaras, had permanent villages on the Missouri where

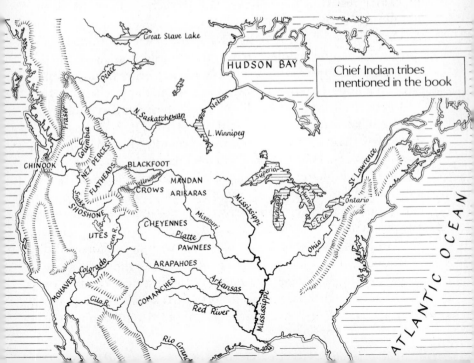

Chief Indian tribes mentioned in the book

*Crow Indians on the move; notice the travois.*

they lived in round earth-covered houses to which they returned in the winter or between hunts. They grew crops, maize, beans, *gourds* and tobacco. Other tribes like the Sioux, the Crows, the Blackfoot and the Cheyennes moved their villages as they hunted.

Their *tipis* were made of buffalo skins. Sewn together, these were stretched over poles fixed in the ground in a circle tilted towards the centre, so they criss-crossed each other near the top. Near the top was a vent for smoke with flaps which were adjusted according to the direction of the wind, so that too much smoke did not blow down into the tent. The Indians often decorated their tents with paintings, usually showing war or hunting scenes. When they wanted to move the Indians took down the tipis, made the lodge poles into a *travois*, loaded them and moved off. This is a traveller's description of an Indian village on the move, crossing a river, three or four feet deep with a swift current:

'For several rods the water was alive with dogs, horses and Indians. The long poles used in pitching the lodges are carried by the horses, fastened by the heavier end, two or three on each side, to a rude sort of pack-saddle, while the other end drags on the ground. About a foot behind the

horse, a kind of large basket or pannier is suspended between
the poles and firmly lashed in its place. On the back of the
horse are piled various articles of luggage; the basket also
is well filled with domestic utensils or, quite as often, with
a litter of puppies, a brood of small children, or a *superannuated* old man. Numbers of these curious vehicles,
traineaux, or, as the Canadians called them, travaux [i.e.
travois], were now splashing together through the stream.
Among them swam countless dogs, often burdened with
*miniature* traineaux; and dashing forward on horseback
through the throng came the warriors, the slender figure of
some lynx-eyed boy clinging fast behind them. The women
sat perched on the pack-saddles, adding not a little to the
load of already overburdened horses. The confusion was
*prodigious*. The dogs yelled and howled in chorus; the puppies
in the traineaux set up a dismal whine as the water invaded
their comfortable retreat; the little black-eyed children,     15

from one year of age upward, clung fast with both hands to the edge of their basket, and looked over in alarm at the water rushing so near them, spluttering and making wry mouths as it splashed against their faces. Some of the dogs encumbered by their load, were carried down by the current, yelping piteously; and the old squaws would rush into the water, seize their favourites by the neck, and drag them out. Stray horses and colts came among the rest.'

But as soon as they were all across, 'in the space of half an hour, arose sixty or seventy of their tapering lodges' on their new camping ground.

These Indians almost lived on the buffalo, using up the whole of him. Buffalo skins made clothes as well as homes. The buffalo's own bones were used to scrape the skins and its brains to soften them. Its sinews provided thread for sewing or to make bow-strings. They used the rib bones to make bows before they started to buy guns from the traders. Needles and chisels were made out of the bones, the horns were used as drinking cups or to hold gun-powder and the bladder became a water bag. Buffalo meat, either fresh or dried, was their main food and if there was no wood, they cooked it over fires of buffalo dung. It was no wonder that these Indians became angry when white people killed the buffalo by thousands, not for food but for hides and horn.

*Indians hunting buffalo.*

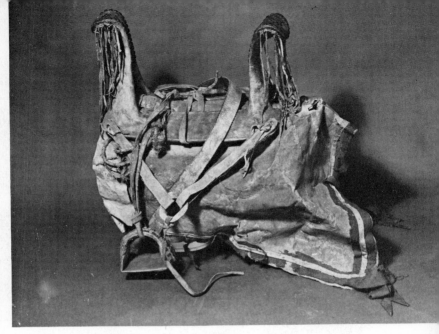

*A Blackfoot saddle; Indians did not always use saddles.*

They were able to live off the buffalo because they had horses to hunt them. The Spaniards brought horses from Europe to Mexico and they spread northwards into the plains, forming herds of wild horses. The Indians were very skilled at breaking them in and riding them. Their children were tied on horses even before they could walk and could ride them by the time they were four or five. Their saddles, if they used them, were made of leather and wood with a high pommel, like those of the Spaniards, and they used only a halter passed through the mouth and round the jaw to guide the horse. They did not look after the horses very well and their backs were often sore from the chafing of the saddles and packs.

They were skilled at stealing horses as well as riding them, especially the Crows, Shoshones and Blackfoot, but most Indians saw nothing wrong in stealing horses from each other or from white people. If trappers met Indians carrying extra halters they knew what they were after. The Indians would set out singly or in bands and either creep up stealthily to cut out

*Blackfoot hide scraper; made out of a flattened gun-barrel.*
*(Right) Blood Indian coup stick; used to touch an enemy to make a coup or in "counting coups".*

a few horses or *stampede* them with wild yells and drive them off
to their own country. Horse stealing or other quarrels could
lead to wars between the tribes. Some tribes were more war-like
than others. One of the fiercest tribes was the Blackfoot, who
were feared by neighbouring tribes and trappers.

Over the Continental Divide on the western side of the
mountains were tribes of a different kind though, like the Plains
Indians, they moved their villages. They sometimes came over
the mountains to hunt buffalo but this usually caused trouble
between them and the Blackfoot. One of these tribes was called
the Shoshone or Snake Indians. The western group of them
lived on meat, roots and berries and used horses, but the eastern
branch which lived in the mountains and dry plains to the
south-west of the Snake river had few or no horses and lived
mainly on roots, seeds and berries with deer or beaver meat
when they could get it. The poorest group of these were the
Piutes or Diggers, called this by the trappers because they lived

on roots, especially the camas root, a lily bulb which they travelled miles to dig. Peter Ogden described a group he met

> 'This appears to be the season of roots in this quarter for all we see are busily employed in Collecting them the bitter and another which would make a good substitute for flour provided it were dried appear to be the most common here, the seed of the sunflowers they also collect for food but the latter does not appear to be very common if *providence* had not given them roots to subsist on six months in the year they would soon perish for want in such a barren country.'

Further south he sees some eating ants and locusts and when he and the trappers were very short of food he consoled himself with the thought that the Piutes were worse off still.

In the plains where the Snake and Walla Walla rivers ran into the Columbia and further north, lived the Nez-Percés or Pierced-nose Indians and the Flatheads. The names were not

*A Nez-Percés papoose carrier.*
*(Right) Blackfoot bow.*

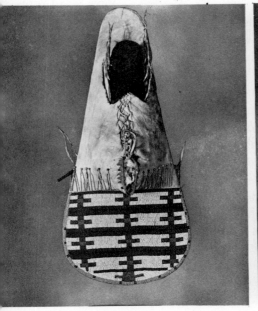
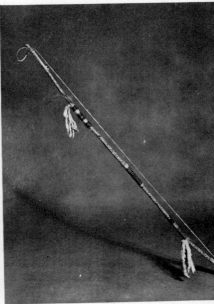

very suitable as the Nez Percés no longer pierced their noses and the Flatheads were called this because they did not, like the Chinooks lower down the river, bind their babies' heads to boards to make them slope back from the nose. These tribes lived partly on salmon from the river and roots and partly by hunting on horseback. The Nez-Percés and their neighbours, the Cayuses, were great horse-trainers and traders. Cayuse became the slang word for a horse because of this. These tribes were very friendly to the white people and were well liked by them.

Farther down the Columbia, nearer the sea, were tribes who led a very different life. They lived mainly on fish, especially salmon. They built *weirs* across the river with gaps through which the salmon had to pass and in the gaps put long cone-shaped baskets made of willow. The fish were caught in these, or sometimes speared by the Indians. Salmon were spread out to dry in the sun or in the smoke of fires and then pounded into powder. This was put into baskets, made of woven bark and grass, lined with dried salmon skin, which were piled in large stacks covered over with mats of rushes. This would then keep for a long time and could be eaten in the winter, or traded for other goods from white traders on the coast or Indians farther up-stream. They ate roots as well, especially the wattapo root, a kind of arrow-head growing in water, with roots the size of a small potato.

They lived in wooden huts, sometimes several families in one long house. The foundations were dug out two or three feet down and a double row of posts about ten feet apart driven into the earth. Overlapping planks were laid between these and the roof was made of planks laid on a ridge-pole. If the house was for several families, separate doors and fireplaces were made. The occupants climbed in stern foremost down a ladder. Their only tools for making these houses were a chisel, a stone mallet and a wedge made of knots of hemlock wood. The door-posts were carved and painted with pictures of men, bears and other animals 'all most hideously unlike nature'. These were the now famous *totem-poles*.

These Indians were skilled canoe-men both on the river and

on the rougher waters of the coast. Their canoes which were sometimes as long as thirty-five feet were made from a hollowed-out tree, with the same tools. No wonder that, when the white traders came, axes were a popular item of trade. They cooked their food in kettles made of cedar wood and grass woven so closely together that they were water-proof. Obviously they could not be put over a fire so they heated the water by dropping in hot stones. The women wore short skirts made of bark and grass and men and women wore robes made of the skins of small animals. These Indians were not so war-like as those of the mountains but they sometimes stole goods, especially those who lived on the Dalles, a long stretch of *rapids* and waterfalls where' traders had to make a *portage*.

The differences in dress and food came about because of differences in land and climate. They also had different social and religious customs though some were similar. In most tribes the men dealt with trapping, hunting, fishing, war, treaty-making and government while the women grew the crops, collected the roots and berries, prepared skins, made clothes, cooked and looked after the children. Children were very rarely punished, at least by beating, because that might break their spirit, but they were expected to help with the *chores* as soon as they were old enough.

As you have seen, many tribes were very skilled in crafts of various kinds. Arikaras were specially good at making glass beads, Crow women were famous for their soft white leather work, decorated with paintings and dyed porcupine quills, and even the despised Diggers could make good baskets. These special skills came in useful for trade when they bartered these goods or sold them for their 'money', which was shells, especially those of the pearl oyster. Shells found on the Pacific often reached the eastern side of the mountains by trade and some Indians who had never seen a white man had their goods which they had traded from other Indians.

Most Indians were fond of decoration. Those at the mouth of the Columbia favoured blue and white beads, plains Indians liked to have coloured cloth or dyed feathers and quills. A German traveller described how the Mandan dandies carried a little mirror attached to their wrists which they would use if they had been travelling on a windy day and wanted to re-arrange their dress. A dandy took great care to work out interesting patterns to paint himself, and if he met somebody who had chosen the same pattern, he would go and change his.

Ways of greeting were the same with most Indians. A blanket waved in the air and then laid on the ground, as though laying down a buffalo robe for a guest, was a sign of peace. Another sign of friendship was to give a belt of *wampum* or smoke a pipe, pointing it first to the sky, the earth and the four points of the compass before smoking it and handing it on to the next man. These international signs were very useful to the explorers and traders because they could use them when they met Indians to show that they meant no harm. Although groups of tribes had different languages, they had a sign language which they all understood.

Most Indians held regular festivals of dancing, feasting and singing like the summer sun-dance of the plains Indians or the buffalo dance of the Mandans. These were to encourage the spirits to help them in their hunting. There was a large number of these spirits who had to be kept sweet by *rites* and sacrifices. Most of the Indians believed in some kind of future life, for which they left goods and food with their dead. They seemed to have thought that the next world would be like this one, but happier because there would always be enough to eat.

The chiefs of the Indian tribes were usually chosen because they were stronger or braver than the others. They did not have much authority over their tribes and would only remain chief as long as the tribe wanted them. The land belonged to the whole tribe and when white people made an agreement with a chief who handed over the land, he had no right to do this and it often caused trouble. When they first met white people, Indians were usually friendly and very helpful as long as they were treated fairly and firmly, as Alexander Mackenzie and Captains Lewis and Clark found. They would guide them, give or sell them food and show them what plants were safe to eat. But when they found the disadvantages of meeting them, they became less friendly. The animals on which they lived decreased in numbers and they were often cheated by traders. White men's diseases like measles and small-pox killed the Indians in large numbers because they were not used to them and did not understand that they had to keep away from people with the diseases to avoid infection. The small-pox epidemic of 1837 killed ninety per cent of the Mandans and it was only one of several epidemics. They began to depend on the white man's tools and weapons instead of making their own, so that they could not do without them. So the traders usually found them ready to sell furs in return for goods without realising the value of what they were selling.

# 4 *The First Traders in the West*

The first white men to trade with the western Indians were Hudson's Bay Company men and the French from Canada. Twenty years after the conquest of Canada a new company was formed by Montreal merchants of American and Scottish birth, the North West Company, which soon began to challenge the *monopoly* of the Hudson's Bay Company.

The two companies were different in many ways. The Hudson's Bay Company had a royal charter and a monopoly of trade in the lands drained by rivers flowing into Hudson Bay which meant the land north of lake Winnipeg and as far west as the Continental Divide. It had a governor and committee in London, and *shareholders* in England; the men who worked in Canada worked for a salary or wages. This table shows the men in Canada in order of importance from the governor down.

Governor

Chief factors

Chief traders

Clerks

*Engagés*

(that is trappers, guides, hunters, boatmen, *interpreters*)

The first four groups were considered gentlemen and called 'Mr.' The engagés were 'men' and called by their surnames. The gentlemen received commissions like army officers, and they and the men were expected to obey their superiors like soldiers. Most of the 'gentlemen' came straight out from Britain and many of the boatmen were Orkneymen, though many were French-Canadians, *métis*, Indians or, after they had started to trade on the Pacific coast, Hawaiians. The Hudson's Bay Company had always traded from forts or trading stations, sometimes called factories, to which the Indians came with their furs. These were usually groups of log huts surrounded by a wooden wall with a gate which could be closed against attack. Later on the bigger forts like Fort William or Fort Vancouver had more extensive buildings.

The North West company traders were mainly Americans, Scots or French-Canadians and many of them did not work for wages but owned shares in the company which gave them an added interest in increasing the profits. Instead of waiting for the Indians to come to their forts, they went to the Indians beyond the Great Lakes, to the Saskatchewan and Athabasca rivers and the Rocky Mountains. The men who went beyond Fort William on Lake Superior were called *hivernants* or winterers, while those who only travelled between Montreal and Fort William were called *mangeurs-du-lard* or pork-eaters.

The traders in both companies travelled in boats or canoes. The York boat was a wooden boat shaped like a *whale-boat* with a crew of six or seven, rowed by oars or dragged by a tracking line in shallow water. It had a mast and sail for travelling on a big lake. The canoes were made of hollowed-out tree trunks or of sheets of birch-bark, sewn with *wattape* and their seams calked with the resin or gum from pine-trees. North canoes were about twenty-five feet long and four to five feet wide and took eight men and two or three passengers as well as goods. The Montreal *canôts de maître* would hold twice as much. They had to be light because there were rapids and waterfalls where the canoes had to be unloaded and carried along beside the river. This was called a portage. Portages could be as long as three or four miles, but might be frequent and short. On his record journey of eighty-four days from Hudson Bay to the mouth of the Columbia in 1824, Governor Simpson's men made a portage at one place of one and a half miles, crossed a swamp a hundred yards across, made another portage of one and a half miles, then rowed across a lake a mile wide, followed by another two-mile portage, a lake half a mile wide, and a two hundred yard portage. Each time the canoe had to be unloaded and loaded again. The boatmen would carry two ninety pound packs, attached to a strap round their foreheads, along these portages by lifts of about five hundred yards, going back for the next load in between.

They got up at two or three in the morning to the cry of 'levé, levé,' stopped for breakfast at eight o'clock, and for their midday meal at one, landed again at eight in the evening and made camp. When they landed they usually carried the *bourgeois* or leader ashore and Simpson described how the smallest man would often, out of pride, carry the biggest bourgeois. On water they averaged six miles an hour and might cover ninety miles a day, cheered on by their work-songs like 'Roulant ma Boule' or 'A St Malo'. Before they arrived at a trading post, they would land a mile or two away, wash and perhaps shave, put on gaudy sashes and feathers in their hats and then sweep up to the fort with a flourish. Some of the Hudson's Bay factors would have a bagpiper to cheer them on their way. Many of the men, especially those employed by the North West Company could not only paddle canoes but build them. The Nor'westers were mainly French or métis familiar with the country and their bourgeois were men born in Canada or America, or determined Scots eager to make a success of their job, especially if they were one of the many partners, when they would get a share in the profits. Although they had a long journey back to Montreal with their furs and although there were often disputes among the partners, their competition soon began to worry the Hudson's Bay Company men, who found that the Indians were intercepted before they could get to their forts.

The North West Company was more ready to encourage their traders to push into new lands in order to expand their trade. The Canadian Rockies and the land on the Pacific were first explored by their men. Alexander Mackenzie tried to find a river flowing to the Pacific and first explored the two thousand mile river now called after him, but he found this flowed northwards into the Arctic. On his second attempt he left Fort Chipewyan in October 1792. He spent the winter on Peace River and then set out again in May 1793, with Alexander

*North canoe carrying Governor Simpson and his piper.*

*Canôt de maître.*

McKay, six French-Canadians and two Indians. The ice on the rivers, the snow in the mountains and the lack of game made it impossible to travel in the winter. As far as Peace River canyon, they travelled on the water but this was one 'white sheet of foaming water' so they had to make a portage which meant carrying the canoe up the mountain by the river side. To do this they made a path by cutting down pine trees so that they all fell in the same direction, still attached to their stumps. A line was fastened to the canoe, and by putting the line round stumps and trees, they would pull the canoe up the almost *perpendicular* slope. They took three days on this portage. There was a longer but easier track behind this mountain followed by the Indians, which Mackenzie should have taken. When he reached the point where the Peace river forked into the Finlay and Parsnip rivers, he followed the Parsnip southwards because an old Indian he met told him that it led to a spot where one day's portage would take them to a great river running to the west. When an explorer was said to have discovered a new route it often meant that Indians told him of one they had used for years.

The portage was more difficult than he expected and Mackenzie found it difficult to make his men go on. He very sensibly

waited till they had a meal, some rum and a fire before trying to persuade them. He reached the Fraser river where he made friends with the Carrier Indians. They warned him of rapids and dangerous Indians on the river, so he decided to turn north-west and travel on an overland trail used by the Indians. There were many Indian villages along the route and at each new village he obtained a guide and finally on 22 July he reached Bella Coola inlet on the Pacific, where he wrote his name and the date on a rock. It is still there, though it has been renewed many times since he first wrote it. At this time, Mackenzie wrote in his journal, 'Our stock was reduced to 20 lb weight of *pemmican*, 15 lb of rice, and six pounds of flour, among ten half-starved men in a leaky vessel, and on a *barbarous* coast.' So they started on their way back often suffering from hunger. After several days of semi-starvation at one time, they shot an elk and 250 pounds of meat were eaten by ten men and a dog between night-time and ten in the morning. On 24 August Mackenzie arrived back at the point where he had started in May. None of his men was killed, none deserted him and they never fired on or killed an Indian: not many explorer-traders could say that. He was the first white man to cross America but he did not find an easy trade route to the Pacific. In 1806

*A portage in 1935; notice the initials on the packing case.*

Simon Fraser explored the river now named after him but found it a dangerous one full of rapids and falls as the Indian had told Mackenzie. David Thompson explored and mapped the upper reaches of the Columbia river. The company wanted

PRO PELLE CUTEM

*The coat of arms of the Hudson's Bay Company. What are the animals? The motto means 'Skin for skin'.*

*The Peace river.*

him to get to the mouth of the Columbia before the Americans, but his men deserted him and he had to winter in the mountains, so that by the time he reached the Pacific he found the Americans already there.

# 5 American Explorers and Traders

The men that Thompson met at the mouth of the Columbia were traders, but the first Americans to get there had been a government team led by Captain Meriwether Lewis and William Clark. Thomas Jefferson had planned this expedition which started soon after the purchase of Louisiana from the French. He wanted them to find a passage to the Pacific, give a full report on the land, the climate, and the Indians on the route and get on friendly terms with the Indians, letting them know that they were now to be governed by the Americans.

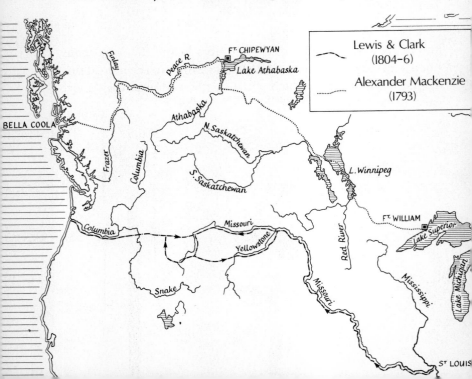

*Alexander Mackenzie.*

Captain Lewis had been preparing for this for some time, studying botany, zoology and surveying and Clark was an experienced frontiersman and a natural geographer. They had read as much as they could of the books written by earlier explorers and had with them Mackenzie's book about his journeys. Both of them were good at dealing with Indians.

Besides the two captains there were fourteen soldiers (all volunteers), nine men from Kentucky, two Frenchmen, an interpreter and a hunter, and Captain Clark's Negro slave, York, whose black skin aroused great interest among the Indians. The interpreter, Toussaint Charbonneau, had with him his Shoshone wife, Sacajawea. He had bought her when she was a child from some Indians who had captured her and, as Captain Lewis wanted the help of the Shoshones in crossing the Rockies, he hoped she would be useful. If they had women with them, the Indians would not think that they were a war

*William Clark.*

party. Sacajawea turned out to be strong and persevering as well as useful.

They set out in May 1804, and travelled up the Missouri to reach the Mandan villages by winter-time. You will find their route on the map. On the way one of their men, Sergeant Floyd, became ill and died. He was buried on a bluff beside the river. They told each new tribe of Indians they met about their 'great father' in Washington and gave the chiefs medals, American flags, fine coats and other presents. When they reached the Mandans where Canadian Nor'westers traded, they warned the Indians against taking medals from the British. They built a fort here and stayed for the winter. The river froze over and the

*Meriwether Lewis.*

snow was too deep in the mountains to go on until the spring. They got on well with the Mandans, visiting their lodges and watching their dances. The Indians also enjoyed watching Lewis's party dance to the tune of the violins they had with them. In February 1806 Sacajawea had a baby son who travelled the rest of the way with them. He was nineteen months old before they got back to the Mandans.

They started again in April, using their boats as far as the headwaters of the Missouri. They had no shortage of food as the country swarmed with animals, including too many grizzly bears to be comfortable. They had many portages, especially a very long one at the Great Falls of the Missouri, where violent storms of hail and thunder caused danger and discomfort. Sacajawea was nearly drowned in a storm when the river rose ten feet within a few minutes.

'Captain Clark fortunately saw it a moment before it reached them, and springing up with his gun and shotpouch in his left hand, with his right clambered up the steep bluff, pushing on the Indian woman with her child in her arms; her husband too had seized her hand, and was pulling her up the hill, but he was so terrified at the danger that but for Captain Clark himself his wife and child would have been lost . . . They had been obliged to escape so rapidly that Captain Clark lost his compass and umbrella, Charbonneau left his gun, shotpouch, and tomahawk, and the Indian woman had just time to grasp her child before the net in which it lay at her feet was carried down the current.'

Some of the men on the plains above had been knocked down by the huge hail stones.

When they reached the point where the Missouri forked into three, they named the rivers Madison, Gallatin and Jefferson, after three American statesmen, and followed the Jefferson. It was now harder to tell which way to go. Until then they had followed the Missouri; now they had to find a route which would take them to a river flowing to the west. They hoped this would not be very far but they needed the help of the Indians to find the best route. Sacajawea now began to recognise some of the landmarks, so they expected to meet the Shoshones. Captain Lewis found them, at last, in August. At first they were very suspicious of him but by signs he persuaded them that he was friendly and they greeted him with hugs which he did not care for much as they were covered with grease and paint. When Sacajawea saw them, she danced with delight, but she found that only a few of her family were left alive.

They realised now that they could go no further by boat so they *cached* their canoes and some of their goods ready for the return journey, bought horses from the Indians and went on through very difficult country over the Lemhi pass into the Bitterroot valley to the Clearwater river. By this time it was September, snow had begun to fall in the mountains, and they found it

*A Mandan village.*

difficult to get enough food. They had many days like this one:
'It began to snow, and continued all day, so that by evening
it was six or eight inches deep. This covered the track so
completely, that we were obliged constantly to halt and
examine, lest we should lose the route. In many places
we had nothing to guide us except the branches of the trees
which, being low, have been rubbed by the burdens of the
Indian horses. The road was, like that of yesterday, along
steep hill sides, obstructed with fallen timber, and a growth
of eight different species of pine, so thickly strewed that the
snow falls from them as we pass, and keeps us continually
wet to the skin, and so cold, that we are anxious lest our
feet should be frozen as we have only thin *moccasins* to defend
them.'

They had to eat some of their horses but they suceeded in
crossing the mountains and reached the Nez Percés Indians in
the Clearwater valley who gave them roots and fish. They were
all sick from this sudden change of diet but this did not prevent
them from building canoes. The river was now deep enough to
carry them down to the Snake and then to the Columbia river,
so they *branded* their horses and left them with the Indians and

went on by water, reaching the Columbia in ten days.

The biggest danger on the Columbia was the rapids, several miles long, called the Dalles. Lewis's party managed to get their canoes down these by some portages and by unloading the goods to be carried by the men who could not swim, while the others shot the rapids. Like many travellers after them, they found that the Indians *pilfered* from their stores if they were not guarded. They now reached the fish-eating Indians who lived in huts. In November they at last reached the mouth of the Columbia and saw the Pacific, or at least as much as they could see of it through the rain that went on for ten days with scarcely a break.

They spent the winter on the coast at the mouth of the river in huts which they built themselves and lived mainly on elk's meat killed by their hunters and fish and wappato roots traded from the Indians. These Pacific Indians were used to white traders who came there by ship and they struck hard bargains with Lewis and his men. He was running short of trade goods especially the blue beads which the Indians valued above everything, and they had to keep some for their return journey. This shortage made them decide to start back in March, though they could not cross the mountains till June. They intended to hunt on their way so that they would not have to buy too much food.

They reached the mountains in May and spent some time there collecting the horses they had left, trading others from the Nez Percés along with roots and meat for supplies. They decided to split up on their way back. Captain Clark was to return the way they had come, as far as the Jefferson, pick up the goods they had cached, strike across to the Yellowstone and go eight hundred miles down that river to the Missouri. Lewis was to go by the more direct route the Indians used to Great Falls, explore the Marias river, go on by boat and meet Clark at the mouth of the Yellowstone.

This plan succeeded but Lewis had two serious mishaps. He met Blackfoot Indians who camped with them. He set a guard at night but he himself went to sleep and when he woke found the Indians making off with some of their guns. He and the men

*Lewis and Clark.*

chased them and, in getting back the guns, killed two of them. The Blackfoot were not friendly anyway, but this made them worse. The second near-disaster was when Lewis was shot in the leg by one of his own men. He was an expert hunter although he was blind in one eye and short-sighted in the other, but this time he mistook Lewis for an elk. The wound was not very serious but Lewis was ill for a time. On 12 August, he joined Clark and the two parties went on down the river. They also met two trappers and John Colter, one of their men, asked and was given permission to return with them on a fur-hunting expedition. At the Mandan villages, Charbonneau decided to stay with Sacajawea and the rest went on down to St Louis where they received a great welcome and a surprised one, as people thought they were dead.

Throughout their journey, they kept detailed diaries describing their route, the weather, the Indians, the landscape, the plants and the animals, and they brought back specimens for Jefferson. They had no desertions after the Mandan villages, and only one (natural) death. Like Mackenzie, they kept on

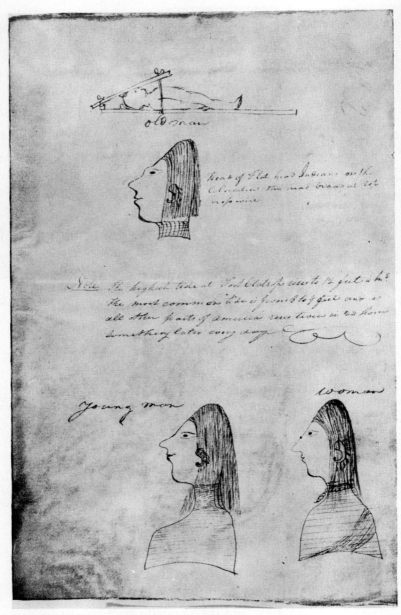

*A page from Lewis's diary; the Clatsops – the real flatheads.*

*Inside a Chinook house.*

good terms with the Indians except for the one clash with the Blackfoot.

In his report on his journey, Lewis wrote that unless American traders went to the Upper Missouri, the trade with the Indians would fall into the hands of the North West Company from Canada. The government should encourage and regulate this trade. The traders did not need much encouragement; they had already traded as far as the lower Missouri and they were ready to carry this trade further. Two companies were in the field soon after Lewis and Clark's expedition: Manuel Lisa's Missouri Fur Company and John Jacob Astor's American Fur Company.

Lisa sent his boats up the Missouri as far as the Yellowstone river but Astor had a more ambitious plan. In 1810 he sent a ship round Cape Horn to the Columbia while a party of men went overland to start a trading post there. The furs they bought could then be sent either back to New York or across to China by ship. The overlanders, led by Wilson Hunt and Ramsey Crooks, raced Lisa's boats up the Missouri from St Louis because they did not trust him and thought he meant to get to the Arikara villages first and persuade the Indians not to trade with them. Hunt meant to go by the same route as Lewis and Clark but he changed his mind when, near the Arikara villages, they met some trappers who turned back with them. These trappers advised them to leave the Missouri at the Arikara villages and cut across the plains on horses to avoid the hostile Blackfoot Indians.

This route turned out to be a good one as far as the Snake river where Hunt and his men thought they could leave their horses and go by boat on the river. They built the boats but they were wrecked in the Devil's Scuttle hole, forty miles of rapids and whirl pools between high cliffs on the Snake. Because of shortage of food they had to split up into groups and continue on foot. After much suffering they reached a camp of the Shoshone Indians who helped them. Some of the men stayed with the Indians but Hunt's group went on to the Columbia, where they found that the party who had come by boat had

*The site of Astoria.*

already built a fort called Astoria and started to trade. Eventually all Hunt's men arrived, except some who had stayed to trap in the mountains.

Next year Hunt went off by ship along the coast to see what trade he could build up there and Robert Stuart, who had come out by boat, went back overland with Crooks and several others. He went by a different route over the mountains, finding a pass in the eastern Rockies called South Pass which thirty years later was to prove the easiest route for wagons over the Rockies and became the main road for settlers crossing the mountains. He arrived back in St Louis in 1812.

Astor's company had made a good beginning, but in 1812 war broke out between the United States and Britain, partly over disputes about land west of the Great Lakes. Many of the men at Fort Astor were British subjects, discontented Nor'-westers who had gone over to Astor's company. They found their position in an American Company in war-time difficult. The North West Company sent one of its traders to persuade the Astorians to sell out to his company which they did, though some of the men did not agree with this and would not work for the North West Company. The post at Astoria was only one part of the trade of Astor's company, so losing it did not mean the end of his fur empire, but for a time he concentrated on the trade east of the Rockies, especially south of the Great Lakes.

# 6 Rival Companies British and American

While the Americans were moving westwards, the struggle for trade between the Hudson's Bay Company and the North West Company had become fiercer. It even broke out into open fighting at times, especially when Lord Selkirk who was connected with the Hudson's Bay Company, tried to start a colony of Scottish Highlanders at Red River, where Manitoba is today. The métis were stirred up by the Nor'westers to attack the colonists, and some men were killed. The Nor'westers built forts near the Hudson's Bay Company forts and tried to persuade the Indians to trade with them. One way of doing this was to trade rum and guns with the Indians and this was bad for both companies. This little war became so serious that the government *intervened* and in 1821 compelled the two companies to *amalgamate* under the name of the Hudson's Bay Company. Most of the Nor'westers worked for the new company, though some went to the United States.

Just before this, in 1818, the American and British governments had made a treaty to settle the boundaries between the United States and Canada. Up to the Continental Divide this was to be the line of 49° *latitude*. They could not yet agree on the land beyond that, called Oregon, partly because it was not well enough mapped, so it was to be open to the traders of both countries for the next ten years, and then it was to be discussed again. In fact the boundary was not settled until 1846. North of the line 54°40′ was Russian territory and south of 42° the land belonged to the Mexicans but the rest was open to the British and Americans.

The Hudson's Bay Company was first in the field. George Simpson, the young and energetic governor of the western

*George Simpson,*
*Governor of the*
*Hudson's Bay Company.*

department, had great plans for the Columbia. He visited it in 1824, and criticised very severely the lack of energy, laziness and extravagance of the traders in the district. He thought that everything there was on too big a scale except the trade. The traders imported too many luxuries, the men wasted too much time hanging about the forts in winter when the animals' fur was at its best. Simpson planned that the district should become *self-sufficient* and the trade should be expanded. He hoped that when the frontier with the States was settled, the Columbia would form the boundary but he did not really expect Britain to keep the land south of the Columbia, so he intended that his trappers should hunt the country bare. This was not the usual policy of the company which tried to *conserve* the animals not *exterminate* them, but here he thought it would be a good way of keeping the Americans out.

45

Fort Vancouver, the Company's headquarters, was moved north of the Columbia, where the Willamette runs into it. Dr John McLoughlin was made chief factor there, and stayed till 1846. Simpson described him as a man he would not like to meet at night in a dark London lane. He was very big and quick-tempered but he was also kind and generous, as many visitors to Fort Vancouver found. He was given instructions to make Fort Vancouver self-sufficient and he carried them out with great vigour. Fifteen years later he had a farm of three thousand acres, ten acres of fruit orchards, flocks of sheep, herds of cattle and pigs, a saw-mill, a corn-mill, craftsmen's work shops, a school, a chapel and a village outside the fort, inhabited mainly by former Company employees. Company ships, including a paddle steamer, took corn south to California and north to the Russian trading posts as well as furs to England.

From this fort McLoughlin governed firmly but fairly the fort itself, the other Company forts farther up the Columbia and along the coast, and the Indians. He supervised the brigades, the canoe loads of trappers who left and came back to the fort, and entertained in a royal style all the travellers who

*Fort Vancouver.*

*John McLoughlin.*

came there. An American traveller here describes dinner at the
fort. When all the guests were seated according to their rank:
'Thanks are given to God, and all are seated. Roast beef
and pork, boiled mutton, baked salmon, boiled ham, beets,
carrots, turnips, cabbage and potatoes, and wheaten bread,
are tastefully distributed over the table among a dinner-set
of elegant *queen's ware*, burnished with glittering glasses and
decanters of various-coloured Italian wines. Course after
course goes round, and the Governor fills to his guests and
friends, and each gentleman in turn vies with him in *diffusing*
round the board a most generous allowance of *viands,* wines
and warm fellow-feeling. The cloth and wines are removed
together, cigars are lighted, and a strolling smoke about the

47

premises enlivened by a courteous discussion of some point of natural history or politics closes the ceremonies of the dinner hour at Fort Vancouver.'

It must have been pleasant for a trapper out in the mountains, down to eating his horses or dogs, to look forward to this.

In spite of all these elegant trimmings, the Hudson's Bay Company was a tough competitor for the Americans. The Indians had looked to it for protection and trade for a long time. Its goods were cheaper and of better quality than those of the Americans. The United States was a new country still trying to build up its industry, so the government put duties on foreign goods which made them dearer, but they did not yet produce enough goods of their own as cheaply as the British. The Indians were shrewd judges of quality and would not accept an inferior article or one without the *trade-mark* they were used to. On the other hand, the Company did not pay very high prices for furs and if the Americans could manage higher prices they might outbid them. In any case, they were ready to try.

In February 1822 this notice appeared in the St Louis newspapers:

*To*

*Enterprising young men*

The subscriber wishes to engage ONE HUNDRED Men, to ascend the River Missouri to its source, there to be employed for one, two or three years —For particulars, enquire of Major Andrew Henry, near the Lead Mines in the County of Washington (who will ascend with, and command the party) or to the subscriber at St Louis.

February 13                    WM. H. ASHLEY

William Ashley was a well-known St Louis merchant, planning to extend the fur trade into the Rocky Mountains. Among the enterprising young men who answered this advertisement and another put in the papers in the next year were Jedediah Smith, of whom you will hear much more, Thomas Fitzpatrick, James Clyman, James Bridger, William Sublette and many others who were to become famous mountain men, well-known even in the eastern States. Ashley intended these men to do the trapping themselves and not just trade with the Indians. He was not at first very successful. In 1822 one of his boats struck a *snag* in the Missouri and sank with its whole load of trade goods, but his chief trader Andrew Henry reached the mouth of the Yellowstone with a group of trappers including Jedediah Smith. Ashley himself went up the river to collect the furs in October and take them back to St Louis while some of Ashley's party spent the winter in the mountains.

Ashley got together more men and boats next year but they met another disaster. They were attacked on the river by the Arikara Indians. Thirteen men were killed and ten wounded, and he had to retreat down the river. Among those who escaped was Jedediah Smith who said a 'powerful prayer' at the burial of some of the dead men. Ashley sent him up to the Yellowstone to fetch help from Henry. He made the journey there and back in a month, and Henry's boats joined Ashley after passing the Arikaras at night. Ashley brought in the army to help but the Captain who led the forces made a treaty with the Arikaras after a very *indecisive* action, to the disgust of the fur traders.

In spite of all these difficulties, Ashley's men got to the mountains overland from the Missouri and separated into trapping parties, in different directions, meeting in 1824 to take the furs down to St Louis. In the autumn of 1824 Smith with six other men crossed the mountains into the Snake River district beyond, where they met some men belonging to a Hudson's Bay Company brigade. This brigade was led by Alexander Ross who had been having trouble with his men. These were mainly French-Canadians, métis and Iroquois Indians, and most of them were freemen. These were trappers who were fitted out with horses and equipment for which they paid the Company, and the Company bought their furs when they returned. Since they had to pay high prices for their equipment and often spent what they got for the furs as soon as they got it, they were usually in debt to the Company. They were a rough lot, 'the scum of the country' according to Simpson the new governor of the Company.

A group of *Iroquois* deserted Ross and went on to trap on

*Peter Skene Ogden.*

their own and had lost their horses and equipment, and their way, when they met Smith's party. They gave him what furs they had in return for helping them to get back to the main brigade under Ross. Ross was suspicious of this story but he let Smith's party travel down to the Flathead Post with him where they stayed some months. Ross had five thousand beaver skins with him but Simpson, who was in the Columbia, decided that a tougher man was needed for the Snake River Country and gave the job to Peter Skene Ogden. This was the summer of 1824 and this was the first meeting between Ogden, the Canadian, and Smith, the American, who were two of the most successful path-finders and trappers of Oregon and California.

Ogden and Smith were both successful leaders of men. They were strong enought to give the unruly ones a *drubbing* if they thought they needed it but they could also win the loyalty of

*Jedediah Smith.*

their men, though it took Ogden some time to get control of his freemen. Both showed the same curiosity to explore unknown country, and both were capable of great endurance. They were well above the average intelligence and education of fur traders. But in appearance and nature they were very different. Smith was very tall, blue-eyed and clean-shaven, with a badly scarred face and ear where a bear had clawed him. Ogden was of only medium height, thick-set and dark. Smith was a very serious-minded young man, deeply religious. He did not drink or gamble as most of the trappers did, though he does not seem to have been hard on those who did. Ogden, on the other hand, had been described by one of his fellow traders as 'the delight of all gay fellows', fond of a joke and a drink. He had been a Nor'wester and was so violent and determined in his opposition to the Hudson's Bay Company that at first they would not 51 employ him after the companies amalgamated. They relented in 1823 and he became a chief trader. Despite his reputation, his journals show that he had a *pessimistic* streak in him. He did believe in a divine providence but he was certainly not as pious as Smith.

Ogden started with one other 'gentleman', a very large brigade of freemen with their Indian wives and children, a smaller number of engagés, 268 horses and Smith's party of seven men who went with him for added protection against unfriendly Indians. Although they were competitors in trade, Americans and British were usually ready to help each other in times of real difficulty and danger. Ogden went along the Bitterroot river and through the Lemhi and Gibbon passes where Lewis and Clark had travelled twenty years before and south across the Snake River to the Bear River district. Smith left him in March to join other Ashley men who were trapping in the mountains. In May, near Bear River, there was a clash between Ogden and a group of American free trappers. Ogden tells the story:

'In the afternoon arrived in Company with 14 of our absent men a party of 25 Americans with Colours flying the latter party headed by one Gardner they encamped within 100 yards of our encampment and lost no time in informing all hands in the Camp that they were in United States Territory & were all free indebted or engaged & add to this they would pay Cash for their Beaver 3½ dollars p.lb & their goods cheap in proportion our Freemen in *lieu* of Seeking Beaver have been with the Americans no doubt plotting.'

The Americans camped nearby and the next morning:

'Gardner came to my Tent & after a few words of no import, he questioned me as follows: Do you know in whose Country you are? to which I made answer that I did not as it was not determined between Great Britain and America to whom it belonged, to which he made answer that it was, that it had been ceded to the latter & as I had no licence to trap or trade to return from whence I came to this I made answer when we receive orders from the

British Government we Shall obey, then he replied remain at your peril.'

When Ogden and Gardner were making these patriotic speeches they were south of the forty-second parallel and therefore both on Mexican soil! These regions had not yet been properly mapped, so they might not have known this, but in any case none of the fur traders paid much attention to the Mexican claims. Ogden was not able to prevent his freemen making off with their equipment and furs but one of them warned him that the others were also planning to *pillage* the camp and by careful preparations and firmness he succeeded in stopping this without any fighting.

Smith was not with these trappers but they may have heard of Ogden's party from him. Ogden was supposed to turn west and explore new trapping country and return by the Willamette valley to Fort Vancouver where the furs could be shipped to England, but, with so many of his men gone, he decided he could not do this. After travelling northwards into the mountains he returned along the Snake River to Fort Nez Percés; from there his 3,000 beaver furs were taken down to Vancouver by boat. He and McLoughlin thought the trouble with the freemen arose because the company charged them too high prices for goods and paid too little for beaver, so McLoughlin altered the prices and Ogden, on his later expeditions, had no more trouble with deserters.

Ogden's deserters, Jedediah Smith and all the other trappers in the mountains, now had plenty of furs but where were they to sell them? Ashley's answer to this question was to bring about a great change in the fur trade. Because of his difficulties in getting boats up the Missouri, he decided to go overland with horses loaded with goods to a meeting place or rendezvous in the mountains where he would exchange the goods for furs. He had a long and difficult journey with the horses and then by the boats his men built to travel along Green river. He arranged the rendezvous on a fork of the Green river and there in the summer of 1825 he did a brisk business with his own men, free trappers like Gardner and Ogden's deserters. This is his account with two of Smith's men:

53

T. Vergel & Isaac Gilbreth

| | |
|---|---|
| 4 Coffee | 6 |
| 3 Sugar | 4.50 |
| 3 Knives | 7.50 |
| doz. hooks | 2 |
| dox. flints | 1 |
| 1½ yds. *Scarlett* | 12 |
| 3 Powder | 6 |
| | — |
| | 39 |

Issac Gilbreth
By 189 lb. Beaver pr. Smith & Co. $567

$3

Thomas Vergil      C.
By 107½      $3      $321.75

This shows that Ashley paid three dollars a pound for beaver but also shows that he charged prices much higher than they were in St Louis. The price for flints in the east was 4 cents a dozen. He had had to bring them a long way from St Louis and there was nobody else competing with him at this rendezvous. A beaver skin weighed about 1½ pounds so that you can work out how many beaver the men had trapped, how much profit they made and also see a slight mistake that Ashley made in their account. These men were Virgin and Galbraith, but spelling was not the fur traders' strong point. These two did not buy very much, but others bought lead, bridles, trap springs, rum, *vermilion*, flour, pepper, tobacco, looking glasses, ribbons, *awls*, needles, tin cups, scissors and shells. Some of these would be for trading with Indians, others for themselves or their Indian wives. Ashley bought 8,829 lb of beaver fur which, back in St Louis, was worth about 45-50,000 dollars. In one year he had made enough to retire from the fur trade, but others carried on the rendezvous every year until 1840.

# 7  *Smith and Ogden, Explorers*

At the second rendezvous, in 1826, Ashley sold his company to his chief brigade leader, Jedediah Smith, and two others, David Jackson and William Sublette. They divided the work between them and Smith was given the task of leading a party to explore the south-west of Salt Lake to see if there was good trapping country there, though he himself thought as much of exploring new land as of getting beaver. Ogden in the same year was going, with the same motive, in roughly the same direction but much farther north. Like many others they believed that there was another great river flowing from somewhere near Salt Lake westwards to the Pacific. They called this the Bonaventure, the river of great adventure, but there is no such river, though they later sometimes gave this name to the Sacramento in California. They did not realise how wide and barren the plains were between Salt Lake and the Sierra Nevada, and how high these mountains were. Smith and Ogden found out the hard way by crossing them.

Smith set out in 1826 along the Sevier river and reached the Virgin river which he called Adams after the President but which later trappers called after Tom Virgin whose account with Ashley you saw. The land near the river was a difficult tangle of hills and valleys which made a later settler say of it that it was a hell of a place to lose a cow. But they got through it to the Colorado river and the villages of the Mojave Indians. These were friendly and traded food for their goods and gave them a guide across the Mojave desert, 25,000 square miles of hot sand, west of the Colorado, with very little water. They crossed the mountains at the other side of the desert by the

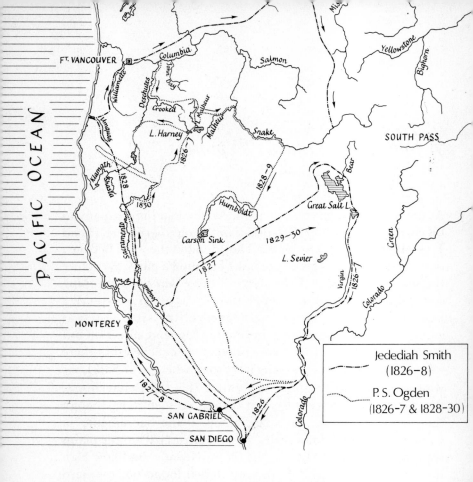

Cajon Pass and travelled down into California to the San
Gabriel mission.

These missions in California consisted of a church, houses,
farm buildings, a big farm with crops and huge herds of cattle
and horses. There were several in California along the royal
road which ran from San Francisco south to Mexico. They
were managed by friars and worked by Indians who had
become Christians. Smith and his men were given a warm
welcome by the friars but the Governor was suspicious of this
band of armed Americans in his country. Smith convinced him
that he was a trader not a soldier but the governor would give
him a passport to leave the country only by the same route he

came. Smith agreed but he did not want to go back by this very difficult route so he turned north into the San Joaquin valley, trapping as they went.

In the spring they tried to cross the Sierra Nevada but he could not find a route among the snow and rocks for a large number of men and horses, so he decided to leave his men to trap along the Stanislaus river and go on with only two men and several horses, find a pass and come back with more men and equipment from the 1827 rendezvous at Great Salt Lake. They succeeded, but it was a terrible journey. They crossed the mountains by the Sonora pass and then struck out across the plains. They had to kill most of their horses for food and nearly died of thirst on the last stretch across the Great Salt Desert, seventy-five miles without water or vegetation. Smith describes this in his journal:

'With our best exertion we pushed forward, walking as we had been for a long time, over the soft sand. That kind of travelling is very tiresome to men in good health who can eat when and what they choose, and drink as often as they desire, and to us, worn down with hunger and fatigue and burning with thirst increased by the blazing sands, it was almost *insupportable*.'

*A Californian mission station like the one which Smith visited.*

One man did give up and they left him, but finding water a few miles further on Smith went back with a kettleful for him which revived him enough to continue. They reached Salt Lake with only one horse and one mule left. They had still six days travel to the rendezvous where Smith wrote, 'My arrival caused a considerable bustle in camp, for myself and party had been given up as lost. A small cannon brought up from St Louis was loaded and fired for a salute.'

He still had to go back to fetch his men in California and ten days later he set out again with a group which included Thomas Virgin and Isaac Galbraith. He took the same route as before to the Colorado, but this time the Mojave Indians were not friendly. They traded with them again but as they were landing after taking their goods across the Colorado on rafts, the Indians attacked. Ten men were killed and Virgin was wounded. The horses were gone and Smith divided what goods they could carry between them and scattered the rest along the bank to distract the Indians. The Indians still followed them, so they took refuge in a clump of trees. They had only five rifles so they fastened their *butcher knives* to long poles to make spears and Smith told them not to fire more than three rifles at first. 'Some of the men asked me if I thought we would be able to defend ourselves. I told them I thought we would. But that was not my opinion.' Smith was wrong because they killed two Indians with the first two shots and the rest ran away. Then Smith and his men had to cross the Mojave desert with no horses and no Indian to guide him this time. He remembered the route but lost his way once, probably because they travelled by night and spent the hot day near the water springs as they had nothing to carry their water in.

Again he travelled into California and joined the men he had left on the Stanislaus river, but he brought few men and no equipment. This time he was not welcome either at the missions or at Monterey, where the governor placed him under guard. He managed to sell the furs his men had trapped in his absence to the captain of a Boston ship in the harbour, but he had to get American and British traders to act as *sureties* for him before he was allowed to leave. He bought a large number of horses

*Part of a page from Smith's journal; thirst in the desert.*

and they got away in December and moved northwards along the Sacramento valley.

At first the trapping was good, although they had few traps left, and they made steady progress; but then Smith decided to cross the Trinity mountains, a maze of canyons and precipices difficult to cross with over 200 horses. When they had crossed he intended to travel along the coast on the beach, but the mountains here came right down to the rocks by the sea so they had to travel along the side of the hills. The Indians were troublesome, stealing axes and knives and shooting arrows at their horses. In July Smith frightened an Umqua Indian into giving up an axe he had stolen by tying him up and putting a cord round his neck. A few days later on the Umqua river, while Smith and two men were away from the camp, the others, for some reason, let the Indians into the camp, which Smith would not have allowed. Suddenly they turned on the white men and killed all except one who escaped into the woods and made his way alone to Fort Vancouver. A day or two later Smith and the two with him arrived at the fort ragged and hungry. One of the men killed was Thomas Virgin.

McLoughlin gave Smith shelter and sent a party under McLeod to recover their possessions and punish the Indians. Smith went with them and they got back some of the horses and equipment but did not punish the Indians, as McLeod considered that the *massacre* had been caused by harshness to the Indians by Smith's men. The Hudson's Bay Company had so much influence in this part of Oregon that they were able to do this without using force. Smith noticed this and wrote to General William Clark that 'until British *interlopers* are dismissed from off our territory, Americans will never be respected or acknowledged as patrons of Indians on the west side of the Rocky Mountains.' But he had no complaints about his own courteous treatment by McLoughlin and Simpson, who was visiting Fort Vancouver while Smith was there. They bought his horses and furs at a reasonable price and he travelled back to the mountains to join his partners, and for the two further years that Smith was senior partner, they did not trap again on the eastern side of the Rockies.

While he was at the fort Smith met Ogden again, back from his fourth trapping expedition. After his first trip, when so many of his men deserted, Ogden had gone on a second expedition to the Snake river district. He met there some of his deserters who were now trapping for the American company. When they heard that the Company now gave better prices for beaver they wished they had not left and one or two came back. In 1826, when Smith was on his way to the Colorado, Ogden went south from Sylvies River to Harney Lake, then east to the Deschutes River and south again to Klamath Lake. All this was new country to him and he did not think much of it. 'This is certainly a barren gloomy looking Country as far as the eye can reach nothing to be seen but wormwood.' His freemen were discontented and he did not blame them, considering their hard life and the small reward they got. At one time they had only six meals in ten days and Ogden wrote: 'This is really a wretched country and certainly no other *inducement* but filthy *lucre* can induce an honest man to visit it, and after all his prospects of obtaining it are most gloomy.'

He seemed to have thought that he would find the Bona-venture, the river of the west, somwhere near Lake Klamath. 'All these waters must discharge to some large River which I hope we shall ere long see.' So he pushed on still further, but there was no river and very few beaver. He convinced himself that the journey had been useful. 'It is however so far satis-factory that we have visited it and the country around us other-wise we as well as others would have remained in doubt regarding it which from our having visited cannot longer remain so and our reward has been two beaver.'

It is to be hoped that this argument also convinced the Company, as he was supposed to be finding beaver, not map-ping the country. Because of the mountains ahead and shortage of food and water, he decided to turn north again, very depressed. 'We have yet three months of Winter God grant they were well over and our Horses escape the kettle but I fear not I truly believe without exception I have been the most unfor-tunate man that ever visited this barren Country the Lords will be done to me situated as I am without a remedy.'

He turned west and crossed the mountains into California as far as Rogue River. There were more beaver here and by the time he had crossed the plains back to Lake Harney and on to Vancouver he had over 2,000 skins but it was still not a very profitable trip.

Later in 1827 he started on his fourth trip to the Snake River district again and spent there the worst winter for years when he was snowed up in his camp with a group of Americans he met. There were no desertions to them this time, though Ogden worried about their influence on his men as they had playing cards with them and alcohol which were not allowed in Hudson's Bay Company trapping brigades, except for the *dram* that Ogden doled out on New Year's Day or at Christmas. He would not sell the Americans snow-shoes to get back to the other trapping parties wintering at Salt Lake, and they had to make their own. Soon after they finally left the camp, they were attacked by Blackfoot Indians and three of them were killed. Some of the Americans thought that Ogden had put the Indians up to this, but it is unlikely. Ogden himself did not think the Americans careful enough in taking precautions against an Indian attack.

In 1828 Ogden returned from the trip to Fort Vancouver, where he met Smith, who had taken refuge there after the Umquas massacre, and heard of his Californian journeys. In the next two years Ogden made two trips in the same direction as Smith and filled in some of the gaps in Smith's maps. This time he went from the Snake to the land north of Great Salt Lake and then westwards to a river which he called Unknown River and his men called Ogden's river, but which was later called the Humboldt after a geographer who had never seen it. Ogden was at a loss to know where this river ran. It actually runs into the desert in Carson *sink*, so Ogden had not found his river running to the west. At Carson sink he was threatened by Indians but he was luckier or better prepared than Smith. A trapper rode back to camp to warn him of the danger. 'They reported upwards of 200 Indians marching on our camp. They came on. Having signalled a spot for them about 500 yards from our camp, I desired them to be seated this order was obeyed.' He saw they were a war party as there were no women or old men with them. They gave him some information about the river and the country to the west. He saw that they had rifles and ammunition and wondered if they had been plundered from Smith's party the year before. 'They requested to be allowed to enter the camp. I refused. A more daring set I have not seen.'

Ogden returned from here as he did not want to 'poach' on the trapping grounds of the Company's Californian expedition. On his last journey in this direction in 1829 he again went to the Humboldt sink where he met Indians who were hostile and would not give him guides. He then turned south and crossed the plains and mountains to the Lower Colorado river. From then on he followed the route of Smith's two journeys to California, but he kept away from the Spanish settlements, probably thinking of Smith's troubles with the Governor and the missions. He trapped the San Joaquin and Sacramento valleys where he met a group of American trappers from Taos led by Ewing Young. With them was a very young man called Kit Carson of whom you will hear again. Ogden travelled with them for ten days to Pit river where he had been on his 1826-7 trip and from there he went back through country he knew. From both these trips they brought back plenty of beaver, but on the last one of his canoes was wrecked at the Dalles with all his papers and journals, so we have no day-to-day description of this trip.

This was Ogden's last trip south of Fort Vancouver. He was transferred to the coast to the north to challenge Russian competition as he had challenged the Americans. Smith too left the mountains in 1830. He sold out his *interest* in his company and invested in a wagon train going to Santa Fé. He went with it and was killed by Comanche Indians. These two men had shown that there was no great river of the west between the Columbia and Colorado but a great area of plains, deserts, mountain ranges and rivers draining inland, not to the Pacific.

# 8 The Mountain Men

While Smith was exploring the west, groups of trappers carried on their trade, turning up, if they had escaped the bears and the Indians, at the summer rendezvous to sell their furs. They came from many different directions, some from the Mexican settlements of Santa Fé or Taos in the south, some from the Hudson's Bay Company forts on the Columbia river to the north-west, some from the Missouri settlements to the east of the mountains, and some from even farther afield. They spoke English, Spanish, French, Indian, or a mixture of all of them. They were different from each other in many ways, but because they were all doing the same difficult and dangerous job, they had a great deal in common.

In dress and equipment they were very like each other. An English traveller, George Ruxton, described a mountain man, as the trappers were called, in this way:

'Williams always rode ahead, his body bent over his *saddle-horn* across which rested a long heavy rifle, his keen gray eyes peering from under the slouched brim of a flexible felt-hat, black and shining with grease. His buckskin hunting shirt, bedaubed until it had the appearance of polished leather, hung in folds over his bony carcass; his *nether extremities* being clothed in pantaloons of the same material (with scattered fringes down the outside of the leg—which ornaments, however, had been pretty well thinned to supply '*whangs*' for mending moccasins or pack-saddles), which, shrunk with wet, clung tightly to his long, spare, sinewy legs. His feet were thrust into a pair of Mexican stirrups made of wood, and as big as coal-scuttles; and iron spurs were fastened to his heel—a bead-worked strap, four inches

*Joseph Walker and his squaw; compare this with the description of Bill Williams.*

broad, securing them over the instep. In the shoulder-belt which sustained his *powder-horn* and bullet-pouch, were fastened the various instruments essential to one pursuing his mode of life. An awl with deer-horn handle, and the point defended by a case of cherry-wood carved by his own hand, hung at the back of the belt, side by side with a *worm* for cleaning the rifle; and under this was a squat and quaint-looking *bullet-mould*, the handles guarded by a strip of buck-skin to save his fingers when running balls, having for its companion a little bottle made from the point of an antelope's horn, scraped transparent, which contained the '*medicine*' used in baiting the trap.'

It may surprise you to know that this man, old Bill Williams, had been a Methodist preacher at one time.

Besides what is described here the trapper would carry in his belt a butcher knife, a *tomahawk* and perhaps pistols as well. On his horse would be his trap-sack containing about half a dozen beaver traps, his 'possibles' sack, in which he carried his *flint and steel*, some ammunition, tobacco and any other small personal property, and a long coiled rope and stake, for *picketing* his horse. On his pack-mules or horses would be packs of the 65 furs he had already collected and spare equipment like a second *lock* for his gun, lead for making bullets, powder, gun-flints or caps, and good, dried meat; near the beginning of a hunt, he would also carry flour, sugar and coffee.

Williams carried a rifle, but some of the men still used muskets which were accurate enough at short range. These were usually flintlocks, though some trappers used the new percussion caps. In the first the powder charge was set off by a flint striking steel, causing a spark to light the powder. The caps contained a special powder which lit when struck a sharp blow. Most of these guns were muzzle loaders and it was no easy job to load them. The gun was half-cocked and a little powder poured into a small pan which was then closed by pulling back the steel. The *butt* of the musket was then dropped down to the ground, powder poured down the barrel and then the ball or bullet inserted and rammed down with a ramrod. The ramrod was a straight metal bar which had to be taken out and fixed back in position under the barrel. You can see why Smith told his men to fire at the Mojaves with only three of their five rifles at first because the Indians could attack while they were re-loading. There are plenty of stories of trappers who did not reload at once and found that the bear that they thought they had killed was only wounded. Most trappers could reload on horseback while chasing buffalo.

A trapper sometimes used the ready-made cartridges, by which the bullet and a measured amount of powder was cased in a leather envelope or he might keep the powder and bullets separate in his horn and shot-pouch. He could make bullets in a bullet mould from melted lead bars. If he put in too much powder the gun might explode. The Indians called Thomas Fitzpatrick 'Broken Hand', because he had lost three fingers when this happened. The Hudson's Bay Company bought most of their guns from Thomas Barnett of London, but the Americans usually used Hawken rifles, Dupont powder and Galena lead from St Louis.

You notice Williams had a bead-worked strap. Some of the vainer trappers would have elaborate bead-work on most of their own and the horse's trappings, decorated pipe cases, feather ornaments and scarlet blankets. Their vanity did not lead them to wash very much, their leather clothes were never cleaned and they wiped their knives on them after skinning an animal. They were often lousy too and their only way of getting rid of the lice was to lay their clothes over an ant hill when they would be eaten clean by the ants.

The beads were embroidered on the leather by *squaws*. Many of the trappers had Indian wives whom they 'bought' in Indian fashion. That is, the trapper went to the father, or nearest male relative of the woman, with a gift of a horse or other property; if the gift was worth enough, the woman was handed over. These Indian women carried in fire-wood, cooked meat, scraped and dressed the skins ready for wearing or selling and so were very useful. They were also expensive, because they liked fine clothes and ornaments and the trappers were expected to provide for their Indian in-laws as well. The American trappers sometimes left their squaws in camps while they trapped, but the Hudson's Bay Company men, who travelled in brigades, often took their wives and children with them. Ogden's Spokane wife went with him.

As long as he kept all his equipment, a trapper could supply himself with food and clothes from the animals he hunted. Fresh buffalo meat was his favourite food. Buffalo could be hunted on foot or on horse-back, when the hunter rode up near to the buffalo and shot it through the spine or lungs. They often killed more than they needed, although their leaders tried to stop them. 'They cannot withstand the temptation of running Buffalo, twenty were killed and not more than the meat of three were brought into Camp this is not only a Sinful waste of meat but also of ammunition,' wrote Ogden.

Cows gave the best meat, especially the lean meat from the hump and back of the buffalo called the 'fleece', the tongue, and the liver which they often ate raw. Soup was made from the blood and marrow bones. The intestines were turned inside out, filled with layers of lean meat and toasted in front of a fire—a much meatier version of our sausage. Trappers thought the world of buffalo meat. They thought it a cure for all diseases and good enough to bring a dead man to life. Eastern travellers enjoyed it as much as the mountain men. Ruxton, planning in England a further visit to the Rockies, wrote to a friend that he was 'half-froze for buffler meat and mountain doins'. Besides buffalo, trappers enjoyed deer meat, beaver tail, mountain sheep, bear and the dogs, specially reared for eating by some Indian tribes.

Sometimes the meat was *jerked,* that is, the lean cut into strips and dried in the sun. Hudson's Bay Company men relied on pemmican. If you would like the recipe for this, you take dried lean meat, pound it into pulp with a wooden flail, put the pulp into a buffalo hide bag until it is half full, stir in an equal weight of melted buffalo fat and perhaps some berries, let it harden and then sew up the bag. They usually made it in 90 lb bags. Other things like hair and stones often got into it and the best that could be said of it was that 'carefully made pemmican, flavoured with berries and sugar, is nearly good', but it would keep a long time.

If fresh or dried meat failed, as they often did, the men went through a time of semi-starvation and then they would eat anything. You have seen how Smith had to kill his horses for food. Sometimes these had died when there was no grass or cottonwood bark for them to eat. When Joseph Walker crossed the Sierra Nevada from east to west, his party lived for fourteen days on nothing but horse meat. Thirst was an even greater danger to those crossing the deserts on the Santa Fé trail or to the east of the Rockies on the way to California, as Jedediah Smith found on the Salt Lake desert. He was searching for water ahead of the main caravan on the Santa Fé trail when he was killed by Comanches.

Cold and wind were great dangers. James Clyman described a winter wind so strong that they could not keep any sort of shelter upright, and so cold that they were too numb to move though they had good buffalo robes. If they could find no wood for the fire, they used sage-brush or dried buffalo dung, but sometimes they could find no fuel at all. In travelling by water, their boats might catch on the snags of driftwood on the wide Missouri or on the rocks of a mountain rapid. In crossing mountains their horses might have to walk on ledges so narrow

*Setting beaver traps.*

that they were in danger of crashing over a precipice, or on 'cut-rock', broken cubes of rock which wore out the horses' hoofs and the men's moccasins.

Few of the wild animals would attack men, but the huge grizzly bear cost some of them their lives. In his diary James Clyman described how Jedediah Smith had his scalp and ear torn by a grizzly. Nobody was very anxious to deal with this. 'None of us having any surgical knowledge what was to be done one Said come take hold and he would say why not you so it went round I asked the Capt. what was best he said one or two go for water and if you have needle and thread git it out and sew up my wounds round my head.' So under Smith's own directions Clyman sewed up the scalp wound and stitched on his ear 'laying the lacerated parts together as nice as I could with my hands'. Clyman adds, 'This gave us a lisson on the charcter of the grissily Bare which we did not forget.'

Illness could be a danger too, as they had few remedies with them and some of these sound worse than the disease. When Ogden's men fell ill from eating diseased beaver meat he dosed them with gunpowder and pepper mixed with water! Surprisingly, they recovered.

Indians were also a danger. Some like the Crows only stole horses or traps but others like the Blackfoot and the Comanches were hostile. You have read how Smith's men were three times attacked by Indians. There are also many stories of individual escapes. John Colter, who left Captain Lewis's party to become a trapper was captured by Blackfoot. They stripped him of all his clothes and equipment and made him 'run for his life', that is they gave him three or four hundred yards' start and then chased him over six miles of prairie covered with prickly pear. Colter was a good runner and escaped all but one Indian who got within yards of him. As he was throwing his spear he tripped and broke it. Colter stabbed him with it and ran for the river. He swam to a mass of driftwood which had settled against an island, dived under it and came up near the middle. The Blackfoot could not find him, and at night he swam down river, landed and then, with no clothes or weapons, living on roots, he walked for seven days to Lisa's fort on the Missouri.

It was always dangerous to travel alone and one of the reasons that Hudson's Bay Company men were seldom attacked was that they travelled in large brigades. Another was that the Company ordered their men (whether they wanted to or not), to keep on good terms with the Indians, while many of the American trappers thought that the only good Indian was a dead one.

To survive all these dangers a trapper had to be tough. They were often as savage as the Indians against whom they fought and would, like them, 'raise the hair' of a dead enemy. They often stayed in the mountains for years at a time. Jim Bridger did not go back to St Louis for seventeen years. The French, though rough, were cheerful and light-hearted, but the Americans were 'watchful, solemn and determined'. They spoke in short sentences and had their own vocabulary which was a mixture of English, French, Spanish and Indian words mixed with a slang drawn from their trade. In talking of themselves, they said 'this coon', 'this hos', 'this beaver', 'this buffler', 'this child' instead of 'I' and at intervals gave the Indian exclamation 'Wagh!' Here is a short 'dictionary' of trappers' language.

rubbed out—killed
gone beaver—dead man
went under—died

raise hair—scalp

on the prairie—free

robe season—winter

doins—food

plug—piece of tobacco

trapper's butter—marrow in bones

meat-bag—stomach

savvy—know

fache—angry

bois de vache—buffalo dung

fandango—a party with dancing

fofarrow—finery

know poor bull from fat cow—know what's what

jornada—a day's journey

count coup—boast of a success

up to the Green river—up to the hilt

bourgeois, booshway—leader

hairy bank-notes, plew—beaver fur

heap—much

if that's the way your stick floats—if that's the way you're
              thinking

half froze for—want very much

Now you ought to be able to translate these sentences:
'Hyar's the doins and hyars the coon who can savvy poor bull
from fat cow', and 'This hos is no b'ar to stick his nose under
cover all robe season'; or this conversation between two trappers
meeting in the mountains:

What's beaver worth in Taos?

Dollar

In Saint Louey?

Same.

H . . . Any call for buckskin?

A heap! The soldiers in Santa Fé are half froze for leather;
and moccasins fetch two dollar easy.

Wagh! How's trade on Arkansas and what's doin to the
Fort?

*Shians* at Big Timber and Bent's people trading smart. On
North Fork Jim Waters got a hundred packs right off and

Sioux making more.

Whar's Bill Williams?

Gone under they say; the Diggers took his hair.

How's powder goin'?

Two dollars a pint.

Bacca?

A plew a plug.

Got any about you?

Have so.

Give us a chaw and now let's camp.

They were great tellers of tall stories, sometimes made up completely, sometimes exaggerations of what they had seen or done. On their travels, some of them had seen fossilised stumps of trees. Before this story had finished going the round of the camp fires, these had become a petrified forest with petrified trees, branches, leaves and petrified birds with their mouths open, ready to sing. Another story was of an echo that lasted eight hours, very useful because you could make sure you woke

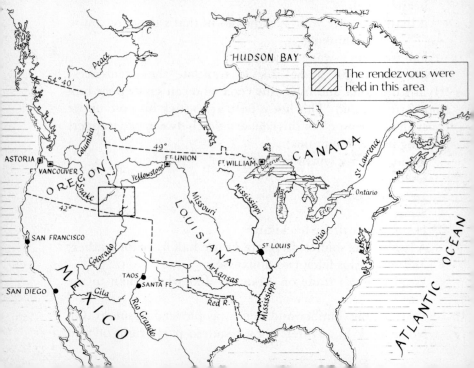

The rendezvous were held in this area

*The rendezvous at Green River, 1837.*

up by shouting 'time to get up' before you went to sleep. Such
stories were told at the winter camps and the rendezvous in
the summer.

The rendezvous were held in different places but the traders
always chose a spot near to a lake or river where there was
plenty of open space with good grass for the horses, and trees
for food and shelter. The towering mountains were always in
sight. The camps covered several miles at the big rendezvous
because many hundreds of trappers, the traders from several
companies and tribes of Indians gathered together. The Indians
dressed for the occasion in their finest clothes, colourful with
beads and scarlet cloth, and paraded in on horse-back. The
men rode over to the traders' camp to sell furs, pemmican and
buckskin clothes made by their women. The trappers often
reached the rendezvous before the pack-train from St Louis and
set up their tents or lean-to's of birch and willow boughs. They
rode out to meet the pack train and, as it came into camp,
pelted hell-for-leather beside it, yelling and firing off their rifles, 73

*The water front at St. Louis; starting point for trappers and emigrants.*

joyful at the prospect of their annual spree. As soon as the goods were unpacked, the goods laid out and the clerks ready, the trappers would move round selling their furs and hearing the latest news from St Louis.

When they had been paid, the noise and bustle increased. Some of the more sober types only visited around the tents of other trappers or swapped stories round the fires, but the others were ready to spend all they had earned, sometimes on necessary equipment but often on fofarrows for their squaws, gambling and whisky. Groups of men played cards or the Indian game of *hand*. There were competitions of horse-racing, running, jumping, wrestling and shooting. The competitors might be sober but were often drunk and blazed away without much regard for the target. Too much whisky often led to quarrels, settled with fist fights or rifle duels in which one or both would be killed. After two or three weeks, the noise of shooting, shouting, barking dogs and neighing horses, the smell of un-washed men, wood-smoke and cooking, the excitement and movement would all suddenly end. The pack-trains moved off on the thousand-odd mile journey to St Louis, the Indians took down their villages and trekked off to their next stop and the trappers loaded up their horses to go back to the mountains. Sometimes they had very little to load up as they rarely saved much and would say 'Thar goes hos and beaver' as their last hairy bank note was spent, and they set off to earn more.

They were not all heedless and savage. Hudson's Bay Company men were often well educated *graduates* of Scottish universities and had a stock of books at their trading posts which they passed on to one another. One American trapper described a winter camp on the Yellowstone.

'There were four of us in the *mess*. One was from Missouri, one from Massachusetts, one from Vermont and myself from Maine. We passed an agreeable winter. We had nothing to do but to eat, attend to the horses, and *procure* firewood. We had some few books to read such as Byron, Shakespeare and Scott's works, the Bible and Clark's Commentary on it and other small works on geology, chemistry and philosophy.'

This might be thought quite hard reading by their descendants today. This letter from Jedediah Smith to his brother does not sound uncivilised.

'I entangle myself altogether too much in the things of time—I must depend entirely upon the Mercy of that being, who is abundant in Goodness and will not cast off any, who call Sincerely, upon him . . . may he, before whom not a Sparrow falls, without notice, bring us, in his own good time, together again.'

One of his fellow trappers said of Smith that 'he was a very mild man and a Christian' but he does add 'that there were very few of them in the mountains'.

# 9 Cut-throat Competition

The exploits of the fur traders and their profits had been reported in the St Louis papers and further east, and in the 1830s many more Americans joined in the search for 'filthy lucre', as Ogden called it. Five of the chief brigade leaders bought up Smith's company in 1830. Thomas Fitzpatrick and Jim Bridger were two of them. They called their company the Rocky Mountain Fur Company. Their chief rival was Astor's American Fur Company, which was still doing well. Its western department was run by Ramsey Crooks who, you will remember, was one of the men who went to Astoria in 1810. His company had bought up its chief rivals on the Missouri, Kenneth Mackenzie's Columbia Fur Company and Pratte, Chouteau and Company, an old French group. The Missouri Fur Company had gone bankrupt. Many of their traders and trappers now worked for the American Fur Company.

The fight between the American Fur Company and the Rocky Mountain Company was rather like the struggle between the Hudson's Bay Company and the North West Company, except that it lasted four years instead of thirty and their men did not actually kill each other. Astor's Company built forts on the upper Missouri to which their trappers and the Indians of the district brought their furs. Fort Union and Fort Mackenzie were in the Blackfoot country and Kenneth Mackenzie was the first to be successful in trading direct with them. When Astor's men joined in the Rocky Mountain trade, they too started to send up pack-loads of goods to the rendezvous, and it was often a race to see whether they got there first or Sublette who supplied the Rocky Mountain Fur Company.

Various smaller companies tried to break into the trade so

that the annual rendezvous became a great mountain fair, with half a dozen companies selling their goods and hundreds of trappers and Indians coming in with their furs. None of these newcomers managed to defeat the two big American companies or the Hudson's Bay Company, though they damaged their trade. In 1832 Nathaniel Wyeth, a Massachusetts ice merchant, had a plan to organise a trapping party in the mountains, to supply goods to the trappers and to send a ship to Columbia to bring back furs and dried fish. But most of his trappers were *green*, his ship was wrecked and Sublette reached the rendezvous with his goods first. After two years of failure, including an· attempt to make a contract to trap for the Hudson's Bay Company, Wyeth sold Fort Hall which he had built on the Snake river to the Hudson's Bay Company and went back east.

Captain Bonneville of the United States army took a large party to the mountains which was given more publicity than any other because a famous American author, Washington Irving, wrote a book about his expedition. As a trader he was no more successful than Wyeth. He built a fort called after him on Green River but did not do much trade there. His expedition is chiefly remembered now because one of his trappers, Joseph Walker, with a large party of men, was the first white man to cross the Sierra Nevada from east to west. He followed Ogden's route along the Humboldt river but crossed the mountains into the Yosemite valley. Both coming and going, his men had a fight with the Digger Indians who were following them and stealing pieces of equipment and many of the Indians were killed. Walker added a good deal to the general knowledge of western geography but he brought back no beaver, some of his men stayed in California and even the horses he bought there died or were eaten on the long journey back, so Bonneville was not best pleased with him.

There were other, smaller companies but they did not have enough *capital* to operate successfully so these were the chief competitors. Most of them were unscrupulous in their attempts to outdo the others. Astor's men, Henry Vanderburgh and Andrew Drips, had less experience of mountain trapping than the Rocky Mountain men, so they dogged the footsteps of Jim

Bridger and Thomas Fitzpatrick to find out where the best trapping grounds were. They also offered very high prices for the beaver and sold goods at low prices. Big companies like Astor's and the Hudson's Bay Company could afford to do this because they were making good profits on other branches of their business and could afford to lose something in the Rockies in order to defeat their rivals. With these high prices they tempted away the trappers from the other companies. Among these were a group of *Delaware* Indians who had travelled with Bonneville. They sold the Indians guns and ammunition which was dangerous because the Indians were as likely to use them to shoot white men as animals or each other. Vanderburgh was killed by a Blackfoot who may have bought his gun from Vanderburgh's own company at Fort Union.

There were many more serious clashes between trappers and Indians in the 'thirties. These were as often started by the trappers as by the Indians, like the 'battle' after the 1832 rendezvous at Pierre's Hole, when a party of traders met some of the Gros Ventres, a branch of the Blackfoot tribe. Godin, a half-breed trapper whose father had been killed by Blackfoot and a Flathead Indian whose tribe had always been their enemies, were sent forward to greet the Gros Ventres chief and shot him dead, though he came with a peace pipe. In the fight that followed several white men and Indians were killed, and some years later a party of Gros Ventres caught Godin on his own and shot him. The trappers sold rum and whisky to the Indians as well as drinking it themselves. Both the United States government and the London governors of the Hudson's Bay company said that alcohol was not to be sold to the Indians, but when the traders were fighting each other for business they all used it. It was watered down to increase the profit but very little rum was needed to make an Indian drunk and they became lazy, diseased and often dangerous if they had too much of it.

The Rocky Mountain Fur Company was not able to keep up its struggle with its wealthy rivals and the partners had to sell out in 1834. Many of their men worked for the American Fur Company instead, but in the five or six years after this the

*Ramsey Crooks.*

mountain trade began to decrease and Astor sold out his shares to Ramsey Crooks. The period of competition helped the free trappers because all the different companies were trying to get their furs. In 1833 they were paid as much as nine dollars a pound for beaver instead of the usual four. This did not last very long but even after 1835 groups of free trappers carried on, taking their furs to the forts after the rendezvous ended in 1840. They were usually very skilled men led by a veteran of the trade and because they knew the country well and needed little capital, they made a fair profit, though some of them spent it as soon as they had it.

More Americans were moving into Mexican territory, where the country had not been trapped so thoroughly. You have heard how some of the trappers went to California. Some Americans had settled in Mexican Texas, and since 1821 Americans had taken wagon-loads of goods along the trail to Santa Fé. Some men started in this trade and then took to trapping for furs along the Gila and Colorado rivers. A good example of these men and of the free trappers was Kit Carson.   79

*Kit Carson.*

As a boy he ran away from the saddler to whom he was apprenticed in Missouri and joined a wagon-train going to Taos. He worked on the wagons for two years and then in 1829 joined a trapping expedition led by Ewing Young to California. On this trip he fought Apaches, suffered from thirst crossing the Mojave desert, helped to track down Indians who stole their horses and met Peter Ogden's brigade in the San Joaquin valley.

After this trip, Carson went north and worked with Bridger and Fitzpatrick and stayed on in the area leading a group. Like these two he had a great reputation as an Indian fighter. None of his fellow trappers were very keen to take him on in a fight either, especially after he killed a *braggart* called Shunar at the 1835 rendezvous. Unlike most trappers he was small and quiet. Ruxton described him as 'Small in *stature*, and slenderly built, but with muscles of wire, with a fair complexion and quiet intelligent features. To look at Kit none would suppose that

*Fort Bridger.*

the mild-looking being before him was an *incarnate* devil in
Indian fight and had raised more hair from the head of Red-
skins than any two men in the western country.' The Indians
called him the Little Chief. Carson could always find trappers
to work with him and when trade became really bad, he signed
on as a hunter at Bent's fort on the Arkansas and combined this
with work as a trapper and guide.

# *10  The End of the Rendezvous*

Why did the rendezvous end? The simple answer is that the fur companies no longer found it profitable to take their pack trains to the mountains to exchange goods for furs, but there is a great deal more behind this simple reason. For one thing the trappers were bringing in less furs because this part of the mountains was 'trapped out'. Nobody was interested in conserving the animals. The Hudson's Bay Company usually did this but it expected to lose Oregon when the boundary was settled so it did not bother, and the competing American companies only wanted to make a profit by killing as many animals as possible. Ogden wrote that it was wasteful to kill female and young beaver as well as males so that there were so few left to breed, but no trap could tell the age or sex of a beaver before it was sprung.

Another reason was that fashions were changing over the other side of the Atlantic. Beaver hats which had been fashionable for two hundred years were being replaced by silk and wool. The new machines used in English factories could make a greater variety of woollen cloth which some people preferred to fur. As less beaver was wanted, the price dropped. Remember the conversation of the mountain men on page 71. This took place about 1846 and beaver was a dollar in Taos. Even if this was a dollar a pound, it would only be about one dollar, fifty cents for each skin, and in 1833 they had been given six. Even before 1840 the American Fur Company had been doing nearly as big a trade in buffalo skins as in fur and others began to join in, so that in the end buffalo became as scarce as beaver.

Some years before the rendezvous ended there were other signs of change. A steam boat chugged up the Missouri as far

"CONTINENTAL"
COCKED HAT.
(1776)

"NAVY"
COCKED HAT.
(1800)

ARMY. (1837)

CLERICAL.
(Eighteenth Century)

(THE WELLINGTON.)
(1812)

(THE PARIS BEAU.)
(1815)

(THE D'ORSAY.)
(1820)

(THE REGENT.)
(1825)

MODIFICATIONS OF THE BEAVER HAT.

*Beaver hats.*

as the Yellowstone river. The mountain trails had been well trodden by the traders and a wagon had been taken over the mountain trails to Oregon. So had cattle. These belonged to missionaries who, helped and guided by the mountain men, made their way to work among the Cayuse and Nez Percé Indians or further on in the settlement of old Hudson's Bay Company men and stray Americans in the Willamette valley. Not only did the missionaries come, but they brought their wives as well and white women appeared at the 1836 rendezvous for the first time. They were frightened by the noise and drunkenness but the trappers were polite enough to them, though they stared very hard. Jim Bridger had not seen a white woman since he left Missouri thirteen years before. Soon after the missionaries, came the first small band of emigrant settlers coming from the States to Oregon. McLoughlin's farm showed how fertile the Willamette valley was and soon more emigrants followed and from 1843 onwards year after year hundreds poured along the trails to Oregon or California. They were encouraged by people like Senator Benton and his son-in-law, John Fremont, who thought that these lands should be added to the United States.

They soon had their way. You have seen already that the American trappers claimed that Oregon should belong to the

*Jim Bridger.*

United States. The treaty of 1818 had been renewed twice, but in 1846 the government in Washington, under President Polk, began to press their claim to Oregon. At first they wanted all of it, but in the end the British and Americans agreed that the boundary should continue along the forty-ninth parallel to the coast, and Vancouver Island should go to Britain. The Hudson's Bay Company still kept some of its trading rights in the area and sold others but later they decided to move to the site of the present day town of Vancouver on the mouth of the Fraser river. One reason why President Polk was willing to give in over Oregon was that the United States was beginning a war with Mexico and they did not want to quarrel with Britain at the same time. They won this war and all the Mexican lands north of the Rio Grande were ceded to the United States, so that California and the south-west lands became part of the States.

# 11 What Happened to the Mountain Men

The American fur trade did not end because the settlers came. It was another fifty years before farmers came in large numbers to western Canada; much of northern Canada is still not settled and they still trap wild animals, though much of the fur comes from animals reared on fur 'ranches'. The Company of Adventurers of England trading into Hudson's Bay still carries on its business, though it deals now in all kinds of other goods besides furs and much of its profits come from big department stores in Canadian towns.

The trappers with the Company went on working for it. Peter Ogden was still a chief factor in the company when he died in 1854. He and James Douglas were in charge of the fort Vancouver after McLoughlin retired in 1846, so he was there when the Americans took over Oregon. His tact made the change smoother than it might have been. The Company was still all-powerful with the Indians in the Columbia and, in 1847, when Cayuse Indians murdered some of the missionaries who had been at the 1836 rendezvous and captured others, Ogden went alone and compelled the chief to give up the survivors. The Hudson's Bay Company was not popular with the American settlers but Ogden was.

The American trappers found it harder to make a living from their trade after 1840 and many tried other jobs. Some became guides. Kit Carson became very famous as guide to John Fremont, a lieutenant in the Army *Topographical* Corps who made several expeditions to the west to find and map routes to Oregon and California. He wrote a book about his first trip in 1843 which became a best-seller and many people in the east heard about Carson because he was Fremont's guide.

Fremont was called the Pathfinder, but it was often Carson and Thomas Fitzpatrick, another of his guides, who found the paths. Carson fought in the war against Mexico in California and later on, after a few years spent in various jobs including driving 6,500 sheep from Taos to Sacramento, he was made an Indian agent by the government.

These agents were responsible for maintaining good relations between the government and the Indians. Most of them were not very successful, as you will know if you have read books or seen films about the Indian wars of the nineteenth century. Oddly enough, Carson, who had so often fought against the Indians, was a good agent. So was Thomas Fitzpatrick who after some years spent guiding emigrants and Fremont, was an agent with the Arapahoes until he died in 1854. An Arapaho chief said that he was the only fair agent they ever had. Carson died soon after the Civil War in which he was a Brigadier General in the *Union* army.

Jim Bridger, 'old Gabe' as he was called by then, built a trading post called Fort Bridger between Green River and Salt Lake which was on one of the emigrant trails to Oregon and California. From there he did some trapping, supplied emigrants and often acted as guide to them. His trading post was not very profitable and he lost it after a dispute with the *Mormons* who claimed his land. He became a guide to the army and to engineers planning the railroads. Though he could not write, he had the whole west mapped out in his mind and people said that if he could not see his way he could smell it. In the last years of his life he went blind and died in 1881.

James Clyman, who, you remember, sewed up Smith's scalp, had retired early from trapping in 1827 and taken up farming in Illinois and Wisconsin. He had served as a volunteer in the Black Hawk war against the Fox Indians in the same company as Abraham Lincoln. He came back to the mountains in 1844 and acted as guide to the emigrants. In 1849, the year of the gold rush, he settled down in California and lived there for the rest of his life. He died in the same year as Bridger but he had a much happier old age as he could still take out his gun occasionally to hunt and he was fond of writing verse, an unusual occupation for mountain men, even when retired.

You remember Ruxton's description of Old Bill Williams. He went on trapping, mainly in the south-west until 1848 when he went as a guide to Fremont on his expedition to the San Juan mountains in Colorado where he was looking for a route for a railroad. Fremont tried to cross them in winter against the advice of the experts. The snow was deep and the Pathfinder lost his way, eleven men died and he had to go back to Taos for a rescue party. He blamed Bill Williams for this, perhaps rightly. Williams came back safely but returned to get some equipment and money left in the snow and was killed, perhaps by Utes. You remember that the trappers said that the 'Diggers took his hair'.

Some trappers took up buffalo hunting or joined in the 1849 gold rush and some, like Clyman, settled down as farmers. But some went on trapping the few beaver that were left, wintering in the lonely valleys high in the mountains and coming to Taos or one of the forts to bring in their furs. They could not bear to leave the free life of the mountains to drive a plough, live in a house and sleep in a bed. Let one of them have the last word.

'It goes against natur to leave buffler meat and feed on hog; and them white gals are too much like pictures and a deal too fofarrow. No, darn the settlements, I say.'

# THINGS TO DO

1   Look up books on costume to find out how the furs were used. C. W. and P. Cunnington, 'Handbook of English Costume' (Faber) is a good one to use.

2   Find an atlas of America with large-scale maps and see how many places you can find named after people mentioned in this book.

3   Find the names which show the people of different nationalities who came to the west. A French and Spanish dictionary will help.

4   Look at the 'trappers' dictionary' again (p. 70), and find out the origin of the words and phrases. Most of the words are explained somewhere in the book. The French dictionary will help again, e.g. *bois de vache* means 'wood of the cow' which means buffalo dung, used instead of wood.

5   Nowadays, governments and voluntary societies try to stop people killing animals like the beaver in large numbers. Find out about nature conservation in Britain and other countries and how you can help in this. A helpful address is The Council for Nature, 44 Queen's Gate, London, S.W.7.

6   Many places mentioned in the book are now National Parks. Find more pictures and descriptions of these places and the plants and animals in them. Some of the parks are the Yellowstone, Yosemite, Three Tetons and Grand Canyon.

7   Find out more about the Indian tribes and their customs and where and how they live now. Oliver la Farge, 'Pictorial History of the American Indian' (Golden Pleasure) is a good source.

8   The Hudson's Bay Company is still a big company in Canada with offices in London. Find out about its activities now.

9   Many firms use the trading methods of the rival companies in the fur trade, e.g. deliberately lowering prices. Try to find some examples of this in shops in your own district.

10   The Indians painted their buffalo-skin tipis with typical scenes from their own lives. Paint pictures for a trapper's tipi, showing scenes from his life.

11   'Tall stories' were the folk-tales of the American West. Make up some tall stories which you think a trapper, a gold-miner or a cowboy might tell.

12   Hudson's Bay Company clerks often came out from Britain to join the company as apprentices of fifteen or sixteen. Imagine you were one of these boys sent overland to Fort Vancouver and write a letter home describing your first impressions of the country.

13   Choose one of the stories in the book, e.g. John Colter's escape, Smith's arrival at Fort Vancouver in 1828, draw a picture to illustrate it and write an 'eyewitness' description.

14 Here are the words and music of the French Canadian boat song, 'Roulant ma boule'. Find others, like 'A St Malo' and 'A la claire fontaine'.

3 En roulant...
   Le fils du roi s'en va chassant, ...
   Avec son grand fusil d'argent.

4 En roulant...
   Avec son grand fusil d'argent, ...
   Visa le noir, tua le blanc.

5 En roulant...
   Visa le noir, tua le blanc, ...
   O fils du roi, tu es méchant!...

6 En roulant...
   O fils du roi, tu es méchant, ...
   D'avoir tué mon canard blanc...

# GLOSSARY

*to amalgamate,* to combine

*awl,* pointed instrument for piercing holes

*barbarous,* wild or savage

*to barter,* to exchange goods

*bourgeois,* leader (special meaning in this book)

*braggart,* boaster

*to brand,* to put a special mark on a horse or cattle with a hot iron

*bullet-mould,* wooden plate with circular holes in which melted lead was poured to make bullets

*butcher knife,* strong knife used by trappers to cut up animals

*butt,* end

*cache,* hiding place (French). A hole was dug in the ground and lined with sticks in which trappers hid their furs or goods if they did not want to carry them further. The soil was carried away to a distance and the turf replaced over the hole so the furs could not be stolen

*camas,* lily plant with a blue flower and an edible plant

*canôt de maître,* master canoe (French)

*Capability Brown,* a landscape gardener in England who designed parks with clumps of trees and pools so that they looked natural.

*capital,* sum of money needed to start and carry on a business

*to cede,* give up

*charter,* written grant of right to trade

*chores,* jobs

*to conserve,* to keep or preserve

*coup,* successful blow or stroke, with real weapons or with stick (p18)

*Delaware,* Indians from the Eastern States, trusted by whites as guides.

*diffusing,* spreading

*dram,* small drink of rum or whisky

*drubbing,* beating

*elusive,* hard to catch

*emigrant,* person who leaves his own country to go to another

*engagés,* man working for wages (French)

*to exterminate,* to root out; kill all

*flint and steel,* sharp stone and metal struck against each other to make a spark to light a fire

*gourd,* kind of climbing plant with large, fleshy fruit

*graduate,* person with a degree

*green,* new to a job

*hand,* Indian game. One man passed a small object from hand to hand quickly, the others guessed which hand it was in. They placed bets on the result.

*hivernant,* trapper who winters out (French)

*incarnate*, in flesh

*indecisive*, with no definite result

*inducement*, reward which persuades a person to do something

*insupportable*, unbearable

*interest*, share in a company

*interloper*, one who interferes in somebody else's business

*interpreter*, person who translates from one language to another

*to intervene*, to come between, interfere

*Iroquois*, Indian tribe from eastern Canada employed as trappers by the Hudson's Bay Company

*to jerk meat*, to cut into strips and dry

*latitude*, distance north or south of the equator measured as part of an angle of 90 degrees. You will find the lines marked on maps

*levé*, get up (French)

*lieu*, place. *in lieu of* means instead of (French)

*lock*, the mechanism of a gun placed between the stock and the barrel, which explodes the charge

*lucre*, money

*to massacre*, to kill a large number of people

*mangeurs-du-lard*, pork-eaters, i.e. fur trader who does not go far enough to live the hard life (French)

*medicine*, a powerful charm, used also as a name for castoreum, the beaver bait

*mess*, group of men who eat together

*métis*, half white, half Indian; a half-breed (French)

*miniature*, small copy of a larger object

*moccasins*, shoes made of deer skin

*monopoly*, the sole right of doing something

*Mormons*, a religious group who settled in Utah and built Salt Lake City

*nether extremities*, roundabout way of saying legs

*occupational disease*, illness people get from the kind of work they do

*papoose*, Indian baby

*pemmican*, dried meat, see page 68 for description

*perpendicular*, very steep, upright

*pessimistic*, seeing the worst side

*petrified*, turned to stone

*to picket*, to put a rope on a horse and tie the rope to a strong metal rod which is driven into the ground

*to pilfer*, to steal

*pillage*, plunder

*portage*, carrying canoes and their loads along the river bank to avoid water-falls, etc.

*powder-horn*, buffalo horn covered over at the end with a stopper in the point, in which trappers kept their gun-powder.

*to procure*, to obtain

*prodigious*, enormous, amazing

*Providence*, another word for God or God's care for people

*queen's ware*, cream-coloured Wedgwood china

*rapids*, part of a river where it ran over and through rocks so that the water was rough

*rite*, religious ceremony

*saddle-horn*, the arched front of the wooden Spanish saddle used by trappers

*sage-brush*, shrub, two to three feet high, with greyish green leaves and blue flowers. It smelled like garden sage

*scarlett*, red flannel cloth

*self-sufficient*, able to look after oneself without help

*shareholders*, people who buy a share in a company in order to share the profits

*Shians*, Cheyenne Indians

*sink*, lake or marsh in which the water of a river sinks through or evaporates

*snag*, piece of sharp timber or drift-wood in a river

*squaw*, Indian woman

*stampede*, sudden scattering of frightened horses or cattle

*stature*, height

*superannuated*, too old to work

*surety*, person who makes himself responsible for another, e.g. to appear in court or pay debts

*temperate*, mild climate; never very hot or very cold

*tipis*, sometimes spelled tepees; Indian tents made of skins

*tomahawk*, a small axe

*topographical*, connected with mapping of landscape

*totem-pole*, Indian door-post carved and painted

*trade-mark*, mark, sometimes a picture, on goods to show who made them

*travois*, sledge made by lashing lodge poles together (see p. 14)

*Union*, the north in the American Civil war

*vermilion*, bright red paint, popular with Indians

*viands*, food

*vieing*, competing

*wampum*, beads made from shells and strung on a string

*wattape*, threads made out of roots of spruce trees, used to sew together bark of canoe

*weir*, fence of stakes across river to trap fish

*whale-boat*, long narrow row-boat

*whangs*, strips of leather

*worm*, corkscrew shaped tool for drawing charge out of gun. The Indians liked them for hair ornaments

*wormwood*, woody herb, two or three feet high with a fragrant smell